Praise for

"After reading *Visioning Onward,* I feel inspired and compelled to share the thoughtful approach to building a collaborative shared vision with colleagues and graduate students. An essential for every principal's desk, this is a practical, purposeful, and action-oriented guide for leaders. Embedded in the context of the book are valuable resources, exercises, and vignettes to aid leadership teams in developing a vision that is encouraging, innovative, and empathetic."

—**Robyn Conrad Hansen**, NAU Assistant Professor
of Practice, National Distinguished Principal,
NAESP President 2015-2016

"The most successful leaders don't get to where they are by accident. They are strategic, purposeful, and visionary. Do you want these characteristics in your repertoire of leadership qualities? Then, grab a cup of coffee and a highlighter, and dig in to this invaluable resource. These three brilliant educators have built a step-by-step process to build, plan, and execute your vision. You won't be disappointed."

—**Adam D. Drummond**, Author & Thought Leader with
the International Center for Leadership in Education

"What a well-conceived book that recognizes how an organized approach to developing a school's vision will work! The authors emphasize the need to allow each school team the freedom to design their own vision. The value of a school's shared vision is stressed, and a systematic process is explained in detail.

Visioning Onward demonstrates the critical need for each stakeholder's voice and the importance this voice is to the acceptance of the developing vision. Included in the book are the potential barriers and a process to ensure sustainability. The authors have devoted an enormous amount of time collecting and creating a wealth of resources, examples, and exemplars. As a career veteran in public education and school leadership, I wish I could have read this before my first principalship! This book is truly an excellent resource."

—**Rich Barbacane**, Office of Overseas Schools,
RavenTek, State Department Liaison for NAESP,
Co-Originator of the World Education Forum, USA,
Past President of NAESP

"Visioning Onward is the right book for any leader who aims to be a visionary champion for their school or organization and bring about transformational change. Co-authors Christine Mason, Paul Liabenow, and Melissa Patschke challenge readers through a series of critical questions, activities, examples, resources, and authentic voices to help us establish a sense of purpose in the way we lead and learn on a daily basis. Each chapter reminds us that it is more than just seeing the vision but doing the work in a way that helps us achieve that vision. This book provides a blueprint to do just that."

—**Jimmy Casas**, Educator, Author, Speaker, Leadership Coach

"Visioning Onward outlines the process and action steps for school leaders to create, share, and implement their vision for a school rather than adopting or adapting someone else's vision. This practical guide is a must-read for all school leaders interested in creating and sustaining a school culture that continues to thrive and responds to changing times and one in which its stakeholders grow. The processes outlined in the book along with the case study examples make this a desk reference for every principal."

—**Paul M. Healey**, Executive Director, PA Principals Association

Visioning Onward

Visioning Onward

A Guide for All Schools

CHRISTINE MASON, PAUL LIABENOW,
AND MELISSA PATSCHKE

Foreword by Daniel A. Domenech

CORWIN
A SAGE Publishing Company

A SAGE Publishing Company

FOR INFORMATION:

Corwin

A SAGE Company

2455 Teller Road

Thousand Oaks, California 91320

(800) 233-9936

www.corwin.com

SAGE Publications Ltd.

1 Oliver's Yard

55 City Road

London EC1Y 1SP

United Kingdom

SAGE Publications India Pvt. Ltd.

B 1/I 1 Mohan Cooperative Industrial Area

Mathura Road, New Delhi 110 044

India

SAGE Publications Asia-Pacific Pte. Ltd.

18 Cross Street #10-10/11/12

China Square Central

Singapore 048423

Publisher: Arnis Burvikov

Development Editor: Desirée A. Bartlett

Senior Editorial Assistant: Eliza Erickson

Production Editor: Tori Mirsadjadi

Copy Editor: Pam Schroeder

Typesetter: Hurix Digital

Proofreader: Susan Schon

Indexer: Sylvia Coates

Cover Designer: Candice Harman

Marketing Manager: Sharon Pendergast

Printed in Canada

ISBN: 978-1-0718-0015-7

This book is printed on acid-free paper.

MIX
Paper from
responsible sources
FSC® C103567

20 21 22 23 24 10 9 8 7 6 5 4 3 2 1

Contents

Note From the Publisher: The authors have provided links to web content throughout the book that is available to you through a QR (quick response) code. To read a QR code, you must have a smartphone or tablet with a camera. We recommend that you download a QR code reader app that is made specifically for your phone or tablet brand.

Scan the QR code above or visit the companion website at
https://resources.corwin.com/visioningonward
to access online resources.

List of Online Resources

To access a list of live links to the following online resources, visit https://resources.corwin.com/visioningonward or scan the QR code above.

Available for download at resources.corwin.com/visioningonward

Foreword

By Daniel A. Domenech

During the course of a given year, I have the opportunity to speak to thousands of superintendents and many more who aspire to become superintendents. My baseline message is as follows: Being a superintendent is the best job in America. No job is more challenging, yet no job is more rewarding.

Today's superintendent must possess the skills, knowledge, and professional networks necessary to succeed. A superintendent must have talents and abilities that extend way beyond the management of curriculum and instruction. In the 24/7 world we live in, a successful school system leader must be an expert politician, an ambassador to the community, and an excellent communicator.

As someone who served as a superintendent for 27 years, I know firsthand how difficult the challenges are, and I'm sure the challenges can be equally as demanding in any leadership position in the field of education.

Our public schools are brimming with innovators—students driven by ideas and dreams. Despite the aforementioned challenges, it's up to us, as educators, to create the pathways and platforms that will make these dreams become reality.

I am so pleased that Christine Mason, Paul Liabenow, and Melissa Patschke have teamed up to create *Visioning Onward*. A myriad of leaders have ideas about where they want to take a system. Here's the potential pitfall: If those ideas are not explained to stakeholders in an efficient way—in a way that they can visualize—the ideas may, in all likelihood, wind up on the scrap heap.

When I was a superintendent, I viewed creating a vision somewhat like an artist painting a picture. By looking at my "canvas," stakeholders would be able to understand what I'm trying to do and where I'm trying to go. The key objective was having staff, faculty, business leaders, community leaders, parents, and students all looking at the same vision, or the same picture, in order to eliminate the possibility of separate interpretations of what my vision was.

My vision focused on making the world a classroom, where learning can take place anywhere. Inside this world, a child would learn at his or her own pace, not in concert with 25 or 30 others. The picture then zooms in on the individual child, not the entire group.

At school districts where I served as superintendent, my vision was always the same. It was comprised of radical changes in how we educate our kids. One of these changes was the offering of full-day kindergarten. I also reorganized classrooms, which meant doing away with rows of desks all facing the front of the room. Some of the approaches may have been different, depending on the district I was leading. Essentially, most of the changes I made exist today.

I recently had a conversation with Bill Belichick, head coach of the NFL's New England Patriots. Belichick is all about vision. He's created a vision for what a successful football team is all about. Even the casual fan wouldn't disagree. Belichick says it's important to communicate that vision to everyone on the team so all the players are on the same page.

What does this boil down to? Creating a vision is critical for the team. You're sending a signal to the community that you're serious about educating today's students, preparing them to lead successful lives beyond high school graduation. By outlining your game plan, you're letting your stakeholders know what they can expect.

Equally as important to creating a vision is to effectively communicate it with the community. No superintendent or principal would argue the importance of getting the support to make your vision a reality. Everyone needs to be on board—teachers, parents, the community, and, most of all, the local board of education.

Time and again, I witness firsthand how successful superintendents create, modify, and tailor the vision to meet the needs of the students they serve. Despite their successes, these "champions for children" are relentless when it comes to fostering their own strengths and improving their craft while making a commitment to making their teams thrive.

In addition, successful school leaders know that a way to bolster their success is to share winning strategies and best practices with their peers. This kind of engagement provides opportunities to learn from one another and build on each other's expertise. I believe the school leader with a shared vision is going to win out over one whose vision is kept behind closed doors.

Whether you're a superintendent, a principal, lead teacher or any other kind of school administrator, there is no greater joy than creating a positive school culture. A dynamic learning community is bound to be the end result. It begins with a successful vision. That's what 21st century learning is all about.

Here's to *Visioning Onward*!

Daniel A. Domenech is the executive director of AASA, The School Superintendents Association.

Preface

The journey into 21st century learning begins with a compelling, collectively developed vision. Whether your school is large or small, rural or urban, high-achieving or struggling, traditional or charter, diverse or homogenous, low socioeconomics or high socioeconomics, visioning is an essential ingredient for success. It clarifies beliefs, understandings, and expectations. A vision shared is a vision that has grown to permit risk, encourage growth, and allow for the expansion of knowledge and experiences.

Visioning Onward will prepare teachers and educational leaders to guide schools through a systematic visioning process. Although our primary audience is school principals, teacher leaders and district administrators will also find value in this book.

In this book, you will learn about the journeys the authors have taken—about our dreams and visions for people and schools in America and around the world. You will hear from exemplary practitioners about their visioning, the processes they underwent to implement changes, and the results of their efforts. Whichever population of students you serve, wherever your school is located, we believe you will find relevant information here.

With *Visioning Onward*, we offer school leaders a stimulating and inspirational resource and a practical guide for creating a vision that transforms schools into 21st century learning environments— environments that strengthen student engagement and cognition, provide safe and nurturing learning opportunities, and produce students who have the skills, knowledge, and dispositions to be successful in their life, work, and community.

We will accomplish the following:

- Point to the why and how for developing a sustainable, yet practical 21st century learning vision for your learning community

- Provide thought-provoking historical information on visioning in education and industry

- Highlight lessons learned about what exemplar schools are doing to turn their visions into reality

- Share the common trends that have emerged across schools and appear to be at the heart of impactful, positive change

- Explain key strategies and tools for clarifying collective beliefs and building a shared vision

- Suggest the use of practical implementation ideas provided from exemplar school leaders

- Provide a case study to further clarify our suggested process

- Contribute insight on breakthrough possibilities that may emerge in the near future

Visioning Onward is designed as a practical guide that will also provide readers with interesting observations about the inspirational visions of major organizations and exemplary schools. In reading it, you will find gems as you learn about how visionary leaders worked with teams to bring about substantive changes to their schools and businesses. We urge you to take the time to marvel at the brilliance at some of the visions we share!

We have organized the book in three sections: Part I—the Historical and 21st Century Foundations for Visioning, Part II—Practical Considerations and Steps to Visioning, and Part III—Visioning at the Macro Level. In Part I, we address the relevance of visioning for schools and the opportunities afforded with Every Student Succeeds Act (ESSA). We also share examples of visions from major businesses such as Amazon, Microsoft, and Starbucks and consider a vision from a global nonprofit organization that works with schools and other organizations, Ashoka. Michael Fullan describes the need for 21st century technology to be "irresistibly engaging and elegantly efficient." We believe these terms can be applied to the visioning process in schools as well. The last thing we need is visioning to be a deadly, mundane exercise. Part I helps set the stage for a provocative look at ways to move successfully into the future.

Part II takes the reader through our proposed Steps to Visioning, with a discussion of considerations for obtaining buy-in from key stakeholders and sustainability. The visioning process we recommend is iterative—we provide a graphic organizer to help guide this process. However, visioning is not always a walk in the park. Sometimes it can be more like climbing a mountain or stumbling over a rock as you strive to gain footing. Like preparing for a hike on the Appalachian or Pacific Crest Trails, principals will be better positioned after learning from others and mapping out their own course ahead of time. In many ways, visioning is like chopping down trees, removing boulders, and clearing brush to forge ahead. Part II will help prepare readers for their journeys by sharing some of the challenges principals faced as they championed their visions while considering the role of their schools within their districts, negotiating with district-level administrators, and building consensus within their school communities.

Part III describes visioning and experience on a global scale as well as challenges and opportunities that exist on the macro level. We end with a discussion of the implications for individual schools and districts.

How to Approach *Visioning Onward*

Principals and others may find it easiest and most straightforward to read this book front to back. That approach will ground you in the context for the book, take you through a step-by-step process, and lead you into future considerations. However, the most will be gained if readers go beyond "reading" this book and fill in the blanks for their own schools and districts. A small study team or core learning team may wish to select a leader and implement the steps we recommend, taking your school through a trial run and preparing for more widespread collaboration with the larger school community, including ways to engage parents and community leaders. Or you may want to begin with a book study group to discuss and learn about what we are recommending before undertaking your own journey.

Whatever approach you take, we believe you will benefit from taking time—time to read, consider, reflect, dialogue, research, and plan. We have captured perspectives on visioning from a diverse group of businesses, schools, and leaders. As you proceed through the book, we try to ask a series of critical questions to guide your reflection. However, even when you are in a reflective mode, you may find that there's a wealth of decisions to be made—with many potential activities (see the exercises at the end of Chapter 3), many models to follow (Chapter 2), and even as you and your team conduct research (Chapter 3), you may find so many options in terms of directions to head. So please, take time to process, find those gems that speak most to you and your team, and piece together a plan (see Chapters 4–6) that best suits your circumstances and needs. The final chapters focus on issues of sustainability and a global view of visioning.

With each chapter, you can count on a connection to the prior chapter, practical exercises, authentic voices, and resources. At the end of the chapters are Practical Points to Ponder and Ideas for Leading and Learning.

We lay out the foundation for visioning and the steps depicted in Figure 0.1 in Chapters 1–6 (you will see this figure again in the concluding chapter as Figure 9.1). In Chapter 7, we provide strategies for sustainability, including how to remove barriers, and lay the groundwork for visions to last beyond the leadership that helped bring a

Figure 0.1   Implementing Your Vision: 8 Critical Steps

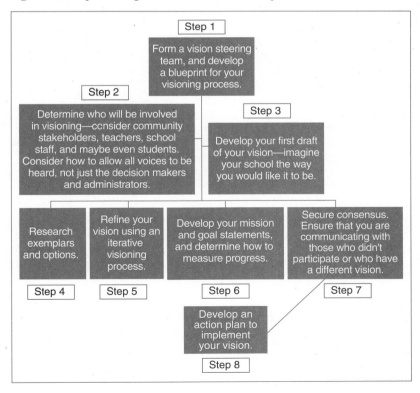

particular vision to the forefront for a particular school or district. However, visioning does not end with Step 8—after that step comes the need for developing a mission statement, goals, and an action plan.

One Size Does Not Fit All

When we review successful schools, whether they are schools that are led by award-winning principals or schools that have received awards from others, a few key things stand out. First among these are that the schools are responsive to their local communities. Yes, many of the most successful schools may demonstrate high academic gains. Many of the most gifted principals have been charismatic. Many of the most successful schools have not had to overcome great adversity. Yet, these schools did not operate rigidly according to a formula that formed a blueprint for allocation of resources, parent involvement, or professional development for staff. Instead, the experts who led these schools had freedom, and with that freedom they worked with teams to design schools that took their schools light-years into the future. In essence, leaders figured out that what worked well in New Mexico may or may not be one of the best approaches in Atlanta.

So, we encourage you to think of shoes. You will have some miles to cover to move ahead. You may want hiking boots, sandals, or a pair of heels. Or perhaps you will do better with wing tips or sneakers. In any event, it is most important that your shoes fit! To get a good fit takes some measurement and comparison—and sometimes trial and error. So, sit down, put on a comfortable pair of shoes, and get ready to take a few steps into your future.

Acknowledgments

Peter Senge and colleagues (2012) in their book *Schools That Learn* say, "Schools that learn are everywhere, at least in people's imaginations" (p. 5). With *Visioning Onward*, we are articulating and advancing the hopes and dreams we have had for schools, for educators, for students—hoping to help advance powerful ideas from points of fantasy to reality. Foremost among those dreams is the vision for schools as empowerment zones. Thanks to Peter Senge and to Peter Schwartz (1996) whose book *The Art of the Long View* guided my work at the Council for Exceptional Children (CEC) as we collaborated with a network of more than 100 educators over several months to develop a plan to address a shortage of teachers of students who are blind. That work and related opportunities at the CEC, at the National Association of Rehabilitation Facilities, and later at the National Association of Elementary School Principals helped us understand what can be accomplished with robust strategies for addressing pressing needs. Thanks also to other well-known educational leaders such as John Hattie, Michael Fullan, and George Couros, who have influenced our thinking and provided such a rich tapestry of perspectives for bringing visions into reality.

A vision, to be fully realized and sustained, is no small thing. On a personal level, thanks to a dedicated team who have encouraged me to stay the course, even when the road became a bit bumpy. To my sister Carol for her understanding of my vision and her eagerness to listen and to share my passion for this work . . . to my friends Atiba Vheir, Lynne Porges, and Maria Livia, for their listening . . . to my yogi friends and colleagues as well as the ancient philosophers and yogis who helped me conceptualize Heart Centered Learning® . . . to a group of former principals and other school leaders who met at least annually with me to reflect on needs and to strategize about the next steps—Paul and Missie were among those, along with Nancy Phenis-Bourke, Kathleen Sciarappa, Mary Woods, Michele Rivers Murphy, Yvette Jackson, Suzan Mullane, and Jill Flanders. A similar thanks to Ingrid Padgett, Monica Jerbi, and Carol Jones, who provided the practical foundational support that was needed to maneuver my way through waters that were sometimes murky. Thanks to my husband John for his love and support, which gave me the space and freedom to pursue my dreams; to our daughters Holly and Amber, who have shared many a dinner as we have considered children, education, and our sacred globe; and to my daughter Maria, who with her related work in the field of mental illness, has shared my aspirations for working professionally to create a more just and caring world.

Chris Mason

Stories, anecdotes, and personal reflections from practicing principals and superintendents make *Visioning Onward* a practical resource for acting and aspiring school administrators. Thanks to Dr. Melissa Usiak, Jennifer Mayes, Mark Terry, and Allyson Apsey for sharing your leadership path to success. Thanks to Dr. Nancy Colflesh and Dr. Debbie MacFalone for your support and positive influence on my personal leadership journey. Thanks to Sean Covey and family for living, modeling, and helping millions set goals, execute with precision, and realize ultimate success.

A special thanks to my wife Bonnie, who has supported my ventures and adventures and joined me in our life's mission: to improve the quality of life for others.

Paul Liabenow

I humbly thank my remarkable coauthors, Dr. Christine Mason and Paul Liabenow, for their patience, guidance, and ongoing belief in my work. Having the opportunity to contribute to this text has been an amazing honor. You have both earned my admiration a million times over. The leadership, networking, and growth opportunities that have been shared with me through my partnership with National Association of Elementary School Principals and the PA Principals Association have been unmatched by any other in my career. The amazing network of school leaders who I now call friends, colleagues, and champions of children are the inspiration of my professional voice. In addition, my appreciation is extended to my college teaching networks through Immaculata University and Neumann University. Many thanks to the Spring-Ford Area School District community and leadership for providing me the platform to practice my trade on a daily basis. The staff of Upper Providence Elementary and Spring City Elementary Schools are second to none. Watching these master educators change lives every day is nothing short of pure inspiration. For every child, now and in generations to come, my wish for each is to have an educational team just as intelligent, collaborative, and loving as those in the Spring-Ford Community. It's an honor to lead, live, and grow in these networks. Finally, I extend my unconditional gratitude and love to my two daughters, Victoria D. Oatman and Olivia M. Oatman. I've had the honor to watch you grow over the past twenty-five years into beautiful, talented, caring young women. Together, you are what fuels my drive to learn and passion to affect our world in a positive way.

Missie Patschke

Our collective thanks to individuals who helped us gather background research, develop ideas, and review drafts along the way, including Dana Asby, Meghan Wenzel, Joanna Marzano, Effie Cummings, June Naureckas, Kristen Hayes, Shu Jie Ting, and Vien Nguyen; particularly to Helen Soule, Aaron Brengard, and Vipin Thekk for their contributions to early drafts of this manuscript; and to Renee Owen, Amber Nicole Dilger, Kevin Simpson, Sharon Kagan, and Ivan Sellers for sharing their insights and advice gathered from their work with visioning.

We also extend our gratitude to the talented team at Corwin—to Arnis Burvikovs, Desirée Bartlett, and Eliza Erickson, and to the production staff at Corwin. Having the opportunity to walk this journey with your expertise and guidance has been valuable to us as educators and as school leaders.

Publisher's Acknowledgments

Corwin gratefully acknowledges the contributions of the following reviewers:

Lisa Graham
Director, Early Childhood Education
Lone Tree, CO

Louis Lim
Vice Principal, Secondary School
Richmond Hill, ON, Canada

LaQuita Outlaw
Principal, Grades 6–8
Bay Shore, NY

Lena Marie Rockwood
High School Assistant Principal
Revere, MA

Karen L. Tichy
Assistant Professor of Educational Leadership
St. Louis, MO

About the Authors

To help you understand how this book came into being and why it is relevant across an array of diverse circumstances, we want to share a little about our partnership.

Christine Mason, Founder/CEO

Heart Centered Learning®—CEI

Established in 2010, the Center for Educational Improvement (CEI) has joined with a number of leaders in mindfulness; science, technology, engineering, arts, and math (STEAM); neuroscience; and social emotional learning to advance 21st century learning in schools. CEI focuses on innovations, building exemplary schools and principals, conducting professional development, and undertaking research to create exemplary learning environments. Heart Centered Learning® is CEI's signature approach to social emotional learning. Heart Centered Learning includes five elements (5 Cs) that lead to compassionate action—consciousness, compassion, confidence, courage, and community. Through these 5 Cs, students become equipped with the knowledge, attitudes, and skills necessary to understand and manage emotions, feel and show empathy for others, resolve conflicts nonviolently, think creatively, and overcome obstacles to succeed in the classroom and in life.

The visioning that is recommended by CEI builds off of Chris Mason's (CEI's executive director) earlier work. From 2011 to 2017, CEI worked with a team of principal leaders to develop our conceptual design for increasing compassion in schools (see Figure 0.2). In 2017,

Figure 0.2   Heart Centered Learning

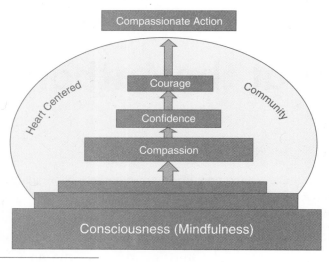

CEI piloted our approach, including an instrument for guiding schools in implementing heart centered visions with schools in Pennsylvania, Massachusetts, and West Virginia. As we worked with these pilot sites, we formalized our process for helping schools implement their visions for 21st century learning in ways that are responsive to the social-emotional needs of students.

CEI is currently expanding our efforts to build compassionate schools. Chris is a coauthor of *Mindfulness Practices: Cultivating Heart Centered School Communities Where Students Focus and Flourish* (Mason, Rivers Murphy, & Jackson, 2018) and *Mindful School Communities: The Five Cs of Nurturing Heart Centered Learning* (Mason, Rivers Murphy, & Jackson, in press), which serve as primers for school leaders to develop mindfulness–compassion protocol. CEI recently conducted a validation study for an instrument we have developed to help cultivate compassionate schools (Mason et al., 2018). The instrument, the School-Compassionate Culture Analytic Tool for Educators (S-CCATE), drives a process for reviewing a school's strengths and needs to begin to consider a vision for a compassionate school. That process is being used as a part of a project with Yale University's Program for Recovery and Community Health and its Childhood-Trauma Learning Collaborative, which Chris is directing.

Paul Liabenow, Executive Director

Principal Mentoring: MEMSPA and the NAESP

The Michigan Elementary Middle School Principals Association (MEMSPA) is currently offering members personal mentoring and professional learning programs as member benefits. Several years ago, MEMSPA realized that its services were being used primarily by white school principals in schools that were also largely white. As executive director, Paul worked with a team of leaders to come up with a vision for improving education in Michigan. To realize the vision, MEMSPA redesigned its programs and offerings to better meet the needs of African American and Latinx principal leaders in urban areas. Today, 20 percent of MEMSPA's members are early career principals, many of whom receive services such as coaching and monthly mentoring chats. Additionally, weekly Tweet chats via #MEMSPAchat have become one of the best education chat experiences in the country. This valuable professional development tool allows like-minded educators to grow their professional learning network far beyond the walls of their schools. Miles disappear as technology provides the path for teachers and school leaders to find ideas, share experiences, and support each other. The motivation of the learning often travels beyond the Twitter format and transforms into emails, phone calls, and even classroom collaborations. With the power of video-based tools such as GoToMeeting and Zoom, educator teamwork is at an all-time high around our country and our world. View **Online Resource 0.1** on our resource page to see an extensive calendar listing of EdChats.

Regarding MEMSPA's current status and where it is headed, Paul says, "We are always visioning—looking ahead and continuously improving." To vision—not only for MEMSPA but for other endeavors focused on mindful practices, social-emotional learning (SEL), and early literacy—requires the collaborative work of leaders who have a heart for improving education for all students. He surrounds himself with business leaders, education content experts, futurists, and trusted allies who share his passion for improving the quality of life for all. A 32-year educator, including nearly 10 years as superintendent of schools, Paul also serves as president of Core Communications International, president of the Center for Educational Improvement, and owner of Liabenow Tree Farms located in Northern Michigan. His experience running a school district as superintendent and several small businesses has helped him develop a network of trusted allies. For his work in education, the visioning group includes principals, university education faculty, and parents.

One of the best ways to understand the value that MEMSPA brings to schools is to talk with a few MEMSPA members. In the pages that follow, you will find five interviews featuring MEMSPA principals that were interviewed for this book.

Melissa Patschke, Principal

Upper Providence Elementary School, Royersford, PA

Spring City Elementary, Spring City, PA

Dr. Melissa (Missie) Patschke has served public education for more than thirty years. She has taught in a variety of special and regular education programs, worked at the middle and elementary levels, and served students from both urban and suburban areas. Missie has hosted national webinars, trained national mentors, and published articles featuring best practices for schools. She has shared her messages on the international platform through exchanges and collaborative projects. She presently serves on the board of directors for the Pennsylvania Association of Elementary and Secondary School Principals and for the National Association of Elementary School Principals. Through these respected networks, Missie partners with leaders across the nation to advocate on behalf of what's right for children and schools. Missie is passionate about shared visionary practices that elevate our impact for children through whole child philosophies, culturally responsive schools, service learning, global networks, mentoring, positive school cultures, and increasing leadership capacity.

PART I

HISTORICAL AND 21st CENTURY CONSIDERATIONS FOR VISIONING ONWARD

Chapter 1

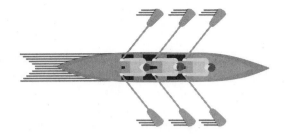

THE ART OF SEEING

Visioning is the art of seeing what is invisible to others.

—*Jonathan Swift*

How Leaders of Learning Transition From Believing It to Seeing It

Our vision is the lens through which we see our world. To make quality systemic changes, we must step forward through what we know is right to what we know is good. Only if we truly believe in the possibility of making a difference will we actually have the tools to make change and empower movement. Vision is the tool by which we show our world what we believe. Our vision extends to the hearts and minds of our schools through the collective networks that share the same beliefs. Thus, many visions and voices become streamlined into a powerful shared vision. This path ultimately illuminates with promise, hope, and passion. This task of multiplexing presses forward with a force unmatched by singular thinking. Students achieve best when schools believe in the potential of their success. Learning is accelerated when there is collective efficacy leading the way (Donohoo, 2016).

If you had all of the resources and power to change something about your school, what would it be? Perhaps higher graduation rates, college enrollment, or attendance? Do you wish for your school to be abundant with learning opportunities for students and for your students to be as excited and inspired to learn as your teachers are to teach? These are powerful and possible visions for schools across the globe, and we are here to provide you with the tools and skills necessary to develop your own vision and transform schools and districts into ideal learning environments where every individual may flourish. In *Visioning Onward*, we will take you on a journey to learn about and prepare for a unique and powerful way of visioning the future of education and the future of your school. We ask you to consider a visioning process that focuses on *the ideal* and an inclusive process of communication, researching options, and broadcasting intent and progress.

If you have ever had a dream for your own destiny, or perhaps even for a few things you want to accomplish in your lifetime, then perhaps you know something of visioning.

Visioning Onward: Preparing for Challenges

In Richard Gerver's provocative book *Creating Tomorrow's Schools Today* (2015), he writes of education as the "platform for our success or failure." Gerver, who Sir Kenneth Robinson (in the foreword to Gerver's book) describes as "one of the clearest and most passionate voices for radical change in education and business," asks whether our children will be prepared for the challenges the future holds. His book lays out a vision for education based on his belief that "classical formal education, based on passing exams, does not produce creative and innovative people prepared for the future . . . [but rather] people who are accustomed to being managed" and often fail "because they expect to be managed" (Gerver, 2013).

In *Creating Tomorrow's Schools*, Gerver (2015) describes how one primary school, Grange, evolved from the brink of failure into a school globally recognized for its success. In 2001, Grange was one of the first primary schools in England to have a wireless network. By 2002, Grange had its own TV station and radio studio. Here's Grange's vision statement:

> Grange Primary school is at the centre of the community, being a happy, inclusive and positive school where everyone (children, staff, parents and caregivers, governors, and the wider community) works together in an effective partnership.

> Our school community ethos is one of mutual respect, understanding and care for all. In everything we do we accept challenges with a positive attitude, always try our best and have the highest aspirations for ourselves and each other.

Children leave Grange as confident, independent individuals with clear dreams and aspirations and the skills, enthusiasm, and sense of self-worth to continue their journey to achieve these and to become responsible, respected, and valuable citizens in our community, our town, and the wider world with strong moral values and beliefs.

(Grange Primary School, n.d.)

Just as Gerver worked with his school community to develop a vision for Grange, your school can be one of hundreds of thousands of schools that can also delve into visioning. Right now, it is the outliers who are seriously engaged in visioning with their schools. Our dream is that more schools will engage their teachers and school communities to take on the exciting and challenging task of visioning as they set about the course corrections we believe are necessary for education in America and around the world.

Collective Visioning

As a school leader, you have the responsibility to always advocate on behalf of what's right for children.

By working with your school team to clarify their collective beliefs and base understandings about what's possible, you are building the capacity of the most powerful influencers in learning . . . teachers (Hattie, 2009).

School vision needs to be shared, directive, relevant, and heart centered. Focusing on the whole child will lead your team to the true power of the passion of teaching and learning.

When we see through the eyes of the learners, we allow them to see our vision of their success.

If they believe it, you'll see it.

What Is the Role of Schools Today?

Gerver's vision was amazing for its time. However, the growth of technology and business concerns since his second edition published in 2015 has been significant. Today, businesses are involved in almost instantaneous ascent or descent, sometimes based on rumors and viral online communications. So, one approach schools could take to develop a vision is to consider Gerver's vision and redefine it within the context of major events and current concerns and capabilities. How could we reconsider "being a happy, inclusive, and positive" school under the context of major current events?

Today, the task of preparing our children to be successful in college, career(s), and as citizens differs greatly from the task before us in 2015, previous decades, or even previous centuries. As the US economy has become more globalized, internet based, and technology driven, many aspects of our lives have changed. Computers and robots now perform many routine and repetitive operations previously done by low-skilled workers. Demand continues to grow for highly skilled workers who can perform complex, nonroutine, analytical functions and transfer skills between jobs as needed (Levy & Murnane, 2005). All the while, artificial intelligence (AI), with intuitive natural interactions and readily available open source tools, grows increasingly more capable of performing complex tasks. AI continues to blur the lines between what humans and machines can do. This shift occurs not only in work environments but also in homes, communities, and schools.

With dramatic shifts in the very nature of work and life, schools face significant challenges to equip students with not only the knowledge but also the skills and dispositions to adapt to the changing economic landscape. Memorizing content and scoring well on tests is no longer a sufficient way of learning. Students need a deeper form of learning that helps them find their place in the world. It is no longer about what we know but what we can do with that knowledge (Fullan, Quinn, & McEachen, 2018). Envisioning this radically different future with the continuing evolution of artificial neural networks is difficult; preparing our students for it is equally challenging.

However, it is not only about preparing students for positive careers and lives as adults. Today, the task of providing positive foundational life experiences for children is growing in importance. More than 6 million young children a year are referred to child protective agencies for trauma due to neglect, physical abuse, or sexual abuse (US Department of Health and Human Services, Administration for Children and Families, 2018). Conservatively, 4.5 million children experience trauma-related obstacles to learning. At the neurobiological level, trauma exposure interferes with the development of a child's stress coping system (Schore, 2001). As a result, development of higher-order cognitive functions is

> Our job is not to prepare students for something. Our job is to help students prepare themselves for anything.
>
> — J. Spencer & A. J. Juliani (2017)

disrupted (Perry, 2001, 2009), leading to considerable anxiety, fear, and obstacles that interfere with learning. Schools need to become a place where students can receive the love and support they may not be receiving at home. It should not only be about cognitive growth but social and emotional growth as well.

The Opportunity That Is Opening for Schools

With the repeal of No Child Left Behind and the passage of the Every Student Succeeds Act (ESSA), states, districts, and schools have more freedom to transform their schools into learning environments that meet today's students' needs. Although some federal requirements such as those around accountability and student achievement remain, an increased focus on developing the whole child and placing responsibility on local institutions has emerged. Schools now have opportunities to define and develop a holistic approach to education. Schools are now given options to measure more than content knowledge and to consider how they want to demonstrate improvements in critical thinking, collaboration, and socio-emotional learning. In this age of accountability, this is a rare opportunity that must be successful if schools are to reshape their educational systems to enable their students to meet the challenges of today and tomorrow.

Rainbow Community School

Renee Owen, Executive Director
Rainbow School
Asheville, North Carolina

Renee Owen, executive director of Rainbow Community School, a private school in Asheville, North Carolina, summed up the priorities for her school this way: "We have a vision of schools as a place where there is co-creation, finding meaning and purpose. We aspire to live with a vision to be in harmony" (R. Owen, personal communication, September 2018).

According to Owen, after forty years, Rainbow has successfully met several of its early goals—the campus has doubled in size, parent engagement is high, and they have a dynamic government system with circles of visioning with students, parents, families, staff, and the community.

At this point, she and other leaders are working to expand the success Rainbow has enjoyed.

Why Visioning?

During the past two decades, external, nonlocal parties have dictated the vision for schools in the United States. For the most part, this has meant that rather than tuning into their inner wisdom, teachers and principals have spent endless hours crafting curriculum pacing guides, prepping students for standardized tests, and developing reports to document their progress. Although it might well be that the vision to raise Trends in International Math and Science Study (TIMSS) and Program for International Student Assessment (PISA) scores and thereby increase our worldwide competitiveness and develop a superior workforce was an excellent vision, what we argue is that when visions are handed to you, or when they come down from on high, an essential element of visioning is lost.

As Simon Sinek (2011) notes, schools are our modern tribes. In your learning community, you have traditions, symbols, and common languages or themes. As a leader, people depend on you to create rules of order and to build a collective vision, purpose, and plan for action. As a school leader, your tribe is depending on you and trusting you, and they will always be willing to work with you once that vision has been articulated through collective knowledge that keeps students' well-being at heart. If vision is handed to you from above, it is your role to take that tool and transform it into a positive, owned belief of how students can achieve in your school.

Imagine a time when you first considered teaching or becoming a school principal. You may have had a vision for your school, for your teams, and for your interactions with students. Now check with your day-to-day reality. Have you been able to realize and sustain your vision? If so, congratulations. How did you do it, and how have you sustained it over a period of time with outside pressures to adjust to changing expectations? There may be lessons you can teach us all. If you have not been able to achieve your vision, we invite you to pause and reconsider what you might do and how you might lead if you had an opportunity to return to a solid vision or to expand upon your current vision. What's possible? How do you trust those in your tribe to contribute to the shared vision? What do you need to let go? What do you believe is right? What more must you do?

The Powerful Impact of Visioning

- **A vision establishes purpose.** Stephen Covey (1989) said it best as the second of his seven habits, "Begin with the end in mind." He goes on to explain that all things are created twice, first as a vision and next as the action. You won't have a product unless you start with the vision. Covey challenges his audience to determine if they'd like to lead by design or by default. Most would choose intentional design as default is a way to ensure eventual failure.

- **Creating a collective vision contributes to a culture of learning.** Gabriel and Farmer (2009) describe a healthy culture "marked by integrity and a strong work ethic. In such a culture, people work across departments and professional roles toward common goals and manage to achieve and sustain success. Staff members are collaborative and reflective risk takers who seek to fix things that aren't working and try to enhance things that are. By flexing their educational muscles, they challenge themselves, their colleagues, and their students. In a healthy culture, educators engage in honest, professional dialogue on curriculum, assessments, data, interventions, and remediation. Participants leave meetings having learned something new, or at least feeling reinforced in what they are doing. They are comfortable with their vulnerability in meetings and view suggestions as constructive, not as put-downs or attacks. Without prompting, they turn to one another when facing a problem or seeking a better way to do something. Their practices are transparent and research-based" (p. 6).

- **Educators who challenge themselves start on a path to growth and improvement.** When working to create a collective vision, schools must challenge themselves to reflect on their own effectiveness, on the impact of the school culture, and on their willingness to grow. Through this work alone, beliefs are challenged, confirmed, and ultimately brought to reality. Frey, Fisher, and Hattie (2018) challenge visionary leaders to embrace mainframes that will maximize student learning. The authors point out that school teams use collaborative dialogue to share their vision. Individuals own their contributions and never retreat to just "doing their best."

- **A shared vision leads directly to collective efficacy.** When a school team embraces the vision that they can move forward, overcome hurdles, and positively affect student achievement, what was once unattainable becomes probable. Fostering collective efficacy among your team should be your number one goal as a leader of learners. Hattie (2016) notes that this factor outranks every other in affecting a child's school success. This includes, but is not limited to, socioeconomic status, home environment, and parental involvement. Fullan and Quinn (2016) note that school leaders who work to create intentional collaborative beliefs about student potential with their teams will make the greatest impact on learning.

Bulldog Tech

Aaron Brengard
Principal, LaVay Tech Middle Schools
San Jose, California

Based on a collective vision shared across the instructional team, Aaron Brengard, former principal of Katherine Smith Elementary School in San Jose, California, described how his team implemented practices to increase student engagement through problem-based instruction and infusion of technology. You can watch a video of Principal Brengard talking about his school's project-based learning journey at **Online Resource 1.1.**

Brengard has recently moved on to be the principal of LeVey Middle School, also in San Jose. At LeVey, Brengard has helped establish Bulldog Tech, a school within a school. Check out the Bulldog Tech website, vision, and goal statement at **Online Resource 1.2.** The Bulldog Tech Vison and Goal statement reads:

Bulldog Tech is a middle school that puts students in the center of their learning. Traditionally, we see students as passive recipients of content in school settings. While this practice may temporarily help to take an annual exam, this type of learning does little to foster the skills or determination needed to make an impact in the world later in life. We believe that in order for students to develop life-long learning, a Constructivist approach, which includes collaboration, critical thinking, social contexts, and real-life experiences, is essential. Combine this approach with rigorous and meaningful situations, guided by our state standards, and it results in learning that lasts longer and goes deeper. Students feel like what they are learning makes sense and they can explain why their learning makes sense.

We know that our students are only with us for two years at Bulldog Tech. And we also know that developmentally, these two years are the most important years in shaping skills and mindsets that will carry on for the rest of their lives. At twelve and thirteen years old, before they head off to high school, our goal is to instill a growth mindset (Agency) in our students that sets them on the path to finding their passion for learning.

Visioning—Permission to Thrive and Change

Michael Fullan, Joanne Quinn, and Joanne McEachen, in *Deep Learning* (2018), ask what we should do if "we want learners who can thrive in turbulent, complex times, apply thinking to new situations, and change the world" (p. 13). They answer that we must "reimagine learning: *what is important to be learned, how learning is fostered, where learning happens, and how do we measure success*?" (p. 13, italics added).

Although there are myriad factors that could contribute to each of these areas, we present a few key ideas:

- *What is important to be learned?*

Every educator has been faced with a student raising his/her hand during a lesson and asking, "Why do we need to learn this?" Educators can view this as a challenge or an element of disrespect, but the reality is that it is truly an excellent question. Learners do need to know why, and so do educators. As a curriculum is developed, school leaders must consider the following:

1. The knowledge and skills to be learned are relevant.
2. Content topics are of interest to learners and to members of their network.

3. The academic content has long-range value.
4. What is learned reflects the common values of the community to ensure success beyond school.

- *How is learning fostered?*

Learning can be considered a biological imperative. Human beings never stop learning. All learners attribute value to the knowledge they acquire—some is lost quickly and some is held for life. When content is valued, it becomes shared. Learners teach others and derive new meaning through application of their learnings.

The amount of individual effort placed in any learning situation is determined by that person's judgment of the value of that investment. Learners do best when academic work is selected, not just expected, to be acquired.

In their book *The New Commonwealth Schools*, Milne and Rhoades Earl (2010) note:

> Students learn best when allowed to choose meaningful projects. Skills are best acquired in a holistic learning environment. Everyone is a genius at something. Everyone has something important to offer. It is impossible to guarantee that all students will learn all the same things. When left alone to explore in a stimulating environment young children are natural learners.
>
> (p. 99)

Collective learning comes through collaborative activities and shared work experiences. Educators guide learners to grow and master understanding in groups.

- *Where is learning happening?*

Sheninger and Murray (2017) identify eight key factors to designing our schools to meet the needs of our future. These authors cry out for urgent attention as a moral imperative to get our schools and students future ready. We are no longer educating today's children for today's concerns. Instead, our work is geared to empower them to learn, to critique, and to apply their knowledge and skills in situations we have yet to understand. We are growing learners, thinkers, and doers, knowing that there is no perfect answer as to how to design schools and learning opportunities. Nor is there one way to do the work. We need to build trusting relationships among those we lead and strive to keep our vision for growth confident yet flexible enough to allow for transformations unknown at this time. This is a most exciting time to be an educator and to be a learner. Opportunities to grow, learn, and contribute to our world are everywhere!

- *How do we measure success?*

During much of the past twenty years, success in schools in the United States was defined in terms of academic success and measured through scores on standardized assessments. Since the passage of ESSA, we are seeing some movement to broaden our definitions of success. Ben Gilpin, principal at Warner Elementary School in Spring Arbor, Michigan, describes how his school has transitioned from solely focusing on academic success to implementing programs that have drastically reduced the number of suspensions and detentions and increased the number of students receiving mental health services.

At the Center for Educational Improvement, we are concerned about school culture and climate, including factors such as student engagement and teacher and student knowledge of self and others. We have developed a tool, the *School—Compassionate Culture Analytic Tool for Educators (S-CCATE)*, which teachers can use to measure compassion and identify areas of needs, progress, and achievement (Mason et al., 2018). It was validated in a study conducted with more than 800 educators and provides a unique tool for examining factors such as equity, understanding of trauma, 21st century learning, neurobiology, metacognition, policy, and principal leadership.

How to measure success? This may be the most pertinent question of all. How do you define success as a school leader? Is it determined by you, by your team, by test scores? There are measures of student learning that are determined often by a collective agreement of skills and required knowledge. Our standards and assessments in formal schooling represent society's agreement of what students should learn, what values to have, and what interests are acceptable.

In the early childhood realm, some of the most important learning takes place during play, exploration, and inquiry (Ontario Ministry of Education, 2014).

Where Does Learning Happen?

Mathew Swoveland (2013), who teaches high-risk students in Massachusetts, in an article on the Teaching Tolerance website, describes how he went out of his way to help a student who only occasionally showed up in his class. In reflecting on the challenges with this student, he concludes that for "some marginalized students, profound learning happens in the space between lessons." Dr. Sandra Rogers (2015), an instructional designer, arrived at a similar conclusion: "During the flow of a task, at the edge of our zone of proximal development (ZPD), via our selective attention, rehearsal, and metacognition is where learning happens."

What if we determined the level of success based on the individual learner's ambitions, goals, and passions?

What if we were able to measure success through a community of learners evaluating the contributions of a collaborative membership?

And, what if success was the outcome of a project, an effort, or an impact that changed a community or socially affected our world?

What if?

Key Learning 1.1

Four Questions From Fullan and Colleagues

Consider your school. At the present time, how would you address the four questions that Fullan et al. (2018) have asked?

What is important to be learned?

How is learning fostered?

Where is learning happening?

How do we measure success?

A New Purpose of Education

After they ask these basic questions, Fullan and his colleagues describe a learning process they call deep learning—and suggest that it must become "the new purpose of education." They ask what an environment "where students truly flourish would look like and feel like?" (2018, p. 13). They urge educators to develop a new vision of education. (We will share more about their vision for deep learning in Chapter 3.)

Would you like to be part of a team that has the opportunity to create a new vision, a new purpose for education? Would your vision be for students to flourish? Would it be similar to the one suggested by Fullan and his colleagues? Would you enjoy having a few extra hours a month set aside for visioning? If you knew it was a priority, could you become excited by the prospects of developing a vision to truly revolutionize education?

Key Learning 1.2

Helping Students Flourish

Helping students to flourish—what would that look like? How would it feel? If you had endless funds at your disposal, what changes would you make? How would you proceed with some confidence that you are on the right path?

Visioning Can Be an Exhilarating Process. If you have ever been with a group that is pioneering a movement, then perhaps you can recall how visioning can help create a sense of purpose and a renewed energy and commitment to improving education. Perhaps for that reason alone it would make sense to bring visioning to schools. Under the right conditions, it can help build staff morale.

Some Additional Considerations—In the Long Term

Consider the "art of seeing." Sometimes we think of visioning as a stimulating, thought-provoking exercise—it certainly can be that. However, as Principal Aaron Brengard has explained, when you are right there in the thick of things, visioning and the implementation that comes after can be grueling. Aaron came on board as the principal at Katherine Smith after six years of declining test scores and enrollment. The vision was first articulated during a summer school program, when Aaron noted a disproportionate number of students lacked engagement, were under-motivated, and needed remedial services. With a team of teachers, he developed a vison for programs that would lead to productive application of academic skills. He saw the potential in the midst of the disappointments, leading his school to adopt project-based learning. Almost like an artist, he crafted a way for the school to make its way forward in the midst of turbulence and trials. Today, the Katherine R. Smith Elementary School (n.d.) has a vision "to be a model of excellence for 21st century learning and community service" and a mission to "prepare each student to think, learn, work, communicate, collaborate, and contribute effectively now and throughout his or her life." Over the past three years, Brengard and a team of leaders have developed procedures to examine their vision and upgrade strategies to reach their goals. In 2017, Katherine Smith School was identified as an exemplary school in the New Tech network.

Staying with a vision in the face of teachers who walk away midstream or pressure from outside forces to go back to the way things were takes conviction and stamina. As Aaron says, "Our school vision keeps my school connected to our purpose—our why. It drives everything we do and helps put us back on our path in times of strain or turmoil" (A. Brengard, personal communication, August 2017).

Key Learning 1.3

Your Experience With Visioning

How would you best describe your experience to date with visioning?

☐ **A Walk in the Park**. It was engaging, fairly easy, straightforward, and helpful.

☐ **Stumbling Over a Rock.** We started out OK, but over time, it seems that we took some missteps. But we picked ourselves up and continued on the journey toward our vision.

☐ **Clearing the Way.** As we continued trying to implement our vision, we kept encountering hurdles to overcome.

☐ **Climbing a Mountain.** It was a difficult, uphill battle filled with differences in opinion and visions and took a great amount of effort.

☐ **Other.** Describe: _____

Conclusions—Visions and Our Day-to-Day Reality

Our visions affect our approach to not only our hopes for our future but also our day-to-day interactions, activities, and even reactions to stress and the disappointments we encounter along the way. When we find ourselves making progress toward our vision, we are likely to experience a sense of delight, and sometimes this even borders on euphoria. For example, with our work toward developing mindfulness and heart centered learning communities, when others are enthusiastic, my colleagues and I revel in a place of bliss, congratulating ourselves on the progress. However, when we hear that teachers and administrators don't have time and can't make this a priority, we find ourselves taking a few dozen deep breaths, reexamining our approach, and reviewing what else can be done. At times, we are even discouraged. Gerver (2013) speaks about helping children prepare for the challenges of the future. Frankly, we find ourselves also constantly priming each other to handle the challenges we face on a daily basis.

Sometimes we wonder about how we might handle the daily stress if we didn't have a vision—our vision helps us persevere. And the power and efficacy of our collective visioning and support is uplifting. One of the ways we keep on going is to examine our indicators of success. We have formal and informal ways of measuring our progress. For us, indicators include things such as the number of requests for more information, the number of adopters, the applause and smiles when we speak, and also the response we receive from experts—those who are informed and already working in our arena. So, whereas visions may provide a lens to the future, the shutter speed, so to speak, is important. We believe in the value of not only peering into the future but also of calculating whether we are staying on course and moving forward.

In Chapter 2, we will advance our argument that visioning has been and continues to be relevant to our lives, to schools, to our understanding of education, and to the future of our children. In Chapter 2 you will learn about the visions of some educational giants as well as the power of having a team and the joy of learning from and with inspirational leaders.

Practical Points to Ponder

- Why do we ask you to consider the "art of seeing?" What talents and skills do artists bring to their canvasses, and why might visioning be compared to the creative process of an artist?

- What are some of the reasons that faculty and staff might have a negative reaction to visioning?

- What additional ideas do you have for helping others set aside any prior negative experiences with visioning?

In this time of relative silence on the national educational front, local leaders have the opportunity to step into the leadership void that is apparent. It is a time when leaders can ask questions about deep learning, questions such as the ones Michael Fullan and colleagues (2018) pose regarding learning—where is learning happening? And measuring success—how should we approach this? How do these questions affect the visions you are already contemplating, even as you realize the value of moving forward at the right time and pace with sufficient support and encouragement from others you trust?

Ideas for Leading and Learning

- Visioning helps us prepare for challenges. What challenges are you facing?

- Do your visions address deep learning? If so, what is your vision for how this deep learning might be measured?

- How can the concept of collective efficacy be used in planning your school's visioning process?

Resources to Explore

Scan the QR Code or visit https://resources.corwin.com/visioningonward to access live links to the online resources referenced in this chapter.

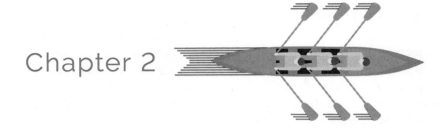

Chapter 2

BELIEVE IT TO SEE IT: CREATING A VISION

Without a vision, our school would be lost in demands, mandates, and knee-jerk reactions.

—*Aaron Brengard, Principal*

What do you believe about progress? What will your school look like in the future? Can you see where you're going? Does your team see the steps to the same journey? Do you believe you can get there? If we can step forward with our end goal in mind, we have a better chance of arrival. If we shift our steps slightly along the way, that's OK. As we learn, we grow; as we grow, we become stronger. The key is to make this journey together as a living system (Covey, 1989). People don't pay attention to what we know; they care about what we do. Therefore, the best visions are embellished by action verbs. Yet, before we can do it, we need to see it. Before we can see it, we need to believe it (Canfield & Switzer, 2005).

Ancient Visions—Burning Cities and Prophecies

Visioning is a process that people have engaged in for a long time. Consider the Greeks with their visions or dreams for their futures and the connection these visions had with Greek mythology. Pregnant with her son Paris, the queen of Troy dreams she gives birth to a burning torch. A seer tells the queen that her son will cause the downfall of Troy. This prophecy becomes reality when Paris's actions prompt the Trojan War. This sort of symbolic dream has not only become a common literary motif but also reflects a reality in which people believed in the prophetic properties of dreams. We can even examine the role of visioning in Greek and Shakespearian tragedies. In these instances, a tragic vision foretells death and misfortune. Yet, in literature, the tragic vision also calls forth human potentiality.

Visioning in Modern Times—Dewey to Today

In more modern times, people have discussed the vision that President Kennedy had for America, the foresight that Steve Jobs had in envisioning the potential for technology, and the vision that is behind so many great inventions. In education, John Dewey, sometimes referred to as the "Father of American Education" or the "Father of Modern Experiential Education," in the 1920s laid the groundwork for progressive 20th century education. Dewey was tireless in advocating for his vision that moved schools beyond being purveyors of knowledge to understanding and supporting students' experiences. In article one of "My Pedagogic Creed" of 1897, Dewey noted multiple educational core concepts that each started with the phrase, "I believe . . ." (p. 77–80). There were many philosophies shared at the time, and whether all agreed with his statements is not relevant. The point here is that he believed them so purely that the foundation of his own values could be seen, shared, and acted on by others.

Some educators even speak of how visions are drivers of change. Peter Senge, a brilliant systems thinker and author of *Schools that Learn*, has a lot to say about visioning. We start with his thought that "aspiration does not come easily in most school settings. It must be deliberately cultivated" (Senge, Cambron-McCabe, Lucas, Smith, & Dutton, 2012, p. 77). We trust that this simple statement, when coupled with Senge's concept that "learning is driven by vision," speaks volumes to a fundamental flaw that has held back many schools. Senge goes further to remind us of the importance of a shared vision. He notes that a community supporting the same vision for learning transforms a school or an organization into a family or a community. Teamwork and common beliefs escalate the power of the whole. Common vision is created by the strongest of leaders. These leaders are able to open the possibilities of the future to their people and allow them to believe in it (Kouzes & Posner, 2009).

Key Learning 2.1

Visionaries

When you think of the word *visionary*, who comes to mind? It could be a historical figure such as Henry Ford, a modern-day technology guru such as Bill Gates, or perhaps someone in your circle of friends. In this exercise, consider the impact of visions for three to four individuals.

Visionary	Visioning	Impact
Steve Jobs	Personal technology	Revolutionized information accessibility & communication

Is Visioning Still Relevant in 2020?

Yes. Of course! Team ISTE (2015) has indicated that the creation of a shared vision is one of the 14 essential conditions necessary to effectively influence technological innovation for learning communities. Every transformational innovation that influences so much of who we are today started with a vision, a dream of what could be. Knowing this, if we are frustrated with the status quo in education and if we want change, then perhaps there is value in delving a little deeper into the visioning process. John Kotter noted in 2011 for *Forbes* that a vision powerful enough to spark change will be communicated in a way that others will "get it." It will be brief, clear, and pointed enough to allow others to buy into it and take action. Transformational leaders know that a vision for change is one that is easy to understand. This has been true historically as well as for today's educators. Believe it and communicate with clarity. Keep it simple; make it memorable.

Why Do We Encourage Schools to Embrace Visioning?

In the past 20+ years, technology and a global economy have significantly changed everything from how we work to how we live.

Preparing students to navigate this constantly changing environment requires new structures, new systems, new technologies, new resources, and new ideas about learning environments.

Jeff Feucht, assistant superintendent at a large school district in Illinois, has championed innovations that increase student engagement in creative ways that build on 21st century technologies. For example, in a recent tweet, he wrote: "Read 180 teachers kicking off a 'book café' where students share their reads from so far this year w students from across district thank you." Could it be that by uncovering and sharing innovations that support the vision and mission of a district (or school), that leaders are not only supporting their vision and mission but also setting the stage for *creating important visions for the future?* Perhaps one of the roles of the district and building-level leaders is to be the catalyst for change to share knowledge and encouragement to help schools and districts examine some of the foremost innovations and promising trends.

Feucht also says there is value in bringing staff together to collaborate with clear purpose that supports the higher calling of the organization. Visioning "alerts everyone in the school to their 'reason for being' and makes it clear where their efforts should be directed" (Bainbridge, 2007).

Feucht, in a review of Michael Fullan's the *Six Secrets of Change* (2011), describes how involving stakeholders in creation of a vision "results in powerful action plans." As Feucht demonstrates, administrators have the power to encourage and stimulate innovation as well as pull people together to create powerful, imaginative, and creative plans for their futures.

Visioning—One Secret of Uncommon Leadership

Debbie McFalone (n.d.), a researcher, author, and thought leader—and the leadership consultant behind LiveWellLeadStrong.com—provided insights into the role of exemplary leaders in inspiring a vision for your school or district (personal communication, 2019). In their landmark research about the five practices of exemplary leaders, Kouzes and Posner (2010), best-selling and award-winning authors, state that leaders who "inspire a shared vision" will sustain a rewarding and successful career over time. Inspiring a clear vision involves encouragement and support, focusing on ownership, and developing commitment to the vision rather than compliance to a plan.

Inspiring a vision for your organization begins with deep knowledge about your own leadership formation—who are you, what do you believe, and what are your guiding principles? Vision for your organization is grounded in that high level of self-awareness. In essence, uncommon leaders declare: "Here's who I am. . . . Now please join me in the way ahead!"

Let's take a look at the three main words in the phrase "inspire a shared vision." To begin, leaders who *inspire* have the capacity to move people through their ongoing encouragement and support. These leaders know the power of capturing uplifting stories and sharing them. They carefully balance elements of support with accompanying accountability, meeting each person where he or she is and taking that performance to a higher level. Indeed, uncommon leaders never hold people accountable until a high level of support has been given for any task. These leaders always ensure time for learning and practicing—therefore their people feel safe and valued. The leader's enthusiasm and clear articulation of purpose engages people with positive energy. And isn't that what we want in our organizations?

A *shared* vision is one in which leaders develop ownership. Rather than being interested in a partnership of mutual understanding, sometimes leaders have a plan in place and then want to "sell" it to others. They risk implementing a top-down model that suppresses innovation, is leader centered, and limits the voices of people in the organization. In today's world, where we truly must have a high level of creativity and collaboration, this approach simply doesn't work.

In contrast, skillful leaders focus on developing mutual *ownership*—a shared sense of vision. Exemplary leaders intentionally engage all voices needed in planning and decision-making—they want to make real progress that everyone will own.

In a large urban school district in southwest Michigan, the superintendent had a clear purpose of moving teachers from isolation to collaboration. The superintendent began to involve people in plans to conduct classroom walkthroughs focused on literacy instruction. The goal was to open up the system and let people learn from their peers as well as share their best ideas. Rather than trying to sell stakeholders, the superintendent involved the teachers' association officers and teacher leaders in the planning from the beginning—these people were literally at the table when decisions were made, ideas were put forward, and goals and outcomes were named for the project. The result? The teacher leaders became advocates for the plan and carried the message of support, growth mindset, and positive adult learning to all teachers in the district. Additionally, literacy instruction improved, and students became more proficient readers.

It Takes a Team

The power of visioning relies on the process used and the engagement of key stakeholders. It is one thing for educational leaders, superintendents, district administrators, or principals to have a vision and quite another for teachers and other stakeholders to embrace that vision. Although rich millionaires or high-tech firms might be able to advance ideas with a one-person show, most often it takes support from others—a team effort—to go beyond the conceptual stage.

In the creation of a team vision, the community elevates trust, and core values are exposed. One of Roy Disney's (n.d.), nephew of Walt's, most famous quotations is a direct reflection of the power of shared vision, trust, and common beliefs, "When your values are clear to you, making decisions becomes easier." Shared vision development is critical to fostering collective efficacy in teachers (Kurz & Knight, 2004). This takes place through building the voice of teachers in cohesive ways. The unity of analyzing beliefs and values bonds teachers in their vision of learning (Donohoo, 2016). Ultimately, this process promises to result in the teachers' visioning through the eyes of the student (Hattie, 2009).

Community Building: How Much Involvement Do You Anticipate?

Imagine that you have joined a local effort to create a community garden. There's been site development, dedicated sponsors, a plot design, and established rules for all volunteers to follow when inside the gates. Hearing of the project, you envision a group coming together to strengthen the community through healthy foods and fellowship. You make a commitment to join this group. As you enter the garden, you are given a work spot and a to-do list. Reading over the instructions, you realize that you may not have understood the purpose of this garden. The instructions ask you to plant squash, peas, and corn. That's all. Just plant these specific seeds in this specific spot. The note thanks you for your time and asks you to return the community tools to the shed before leaving.

Lost in your thoughts, you realize you were hoping for the opportunity to grow fresh tomatoes, cucumbers, green beans, and perhaps even some raspberries. You've done this before with great success. Your mind drifts further, and you wonder if a compost plan has been designed. You gaze at the property fencing and see the potential of planting flowers or shrubs at the garden's edges to promote goodwill with non-gardening neighbors and those passing by. Finally, children come to mind. Is this a place where children can learn, harvest, and share the bounty of the earth? Could there be a special spot set aside for them to explore at their own speed? Finally, how will you share these ideas with fellow gardeners? Who makes these decisions? Can we begin an e-mail list or hang an onsite rainproof bulletin board, and would it be possible to have regular meetings or celebrations of our accomplishments?

Can you imagine looking forward to tending fresh cucumbers and tomatoes while expecting to share the experience with others but instead spending hours on end tending a garden that raises squash and peas with no explanation of why or what the importance of these efforts would produce?

Key Learning 2.2

Creating Your School Garden

Let's apply this metaphor to your school or district. What might you want to plant? Are you considering book cafés as suggested by Jeff Feucht? Will there be Chromebooks or iPads? Is there a community service project that is just waiting for your school's support? What seeds do you want to plant? How could you get input from your community of teachers, staff, and families? Who's interested? Who should be on your planning committee? Where will you get the resources you need? Is there someone or a group that you need to ask permission? What's the timeline for growth? Which areas will need different levels of attention? How will you organize your garden and the efforts that contribute to its success? How will children in your garden have a voice and contribute to their own growth? What rules are needed to ensure that fellow gardeners get along well and communication is a high priority? Finally, your school garden is about strengthening the students, the staff, and the greater school family. How will you ensure everyone is an active participant? How will you share your growth, capitalize on your successes, and celebrate all that's right? How will you make sure everyone knows the collective "why"?

If you want buy-in and support, make sure that your team has input. Perhaps you can recall a time when someone who was influential in your life simply assumed you would, of course, value highly that person's vision. It may be a parent's vision that you will be a virtuoso violinist or soccer star or perhaps a friend's vision for an upcoming trip abroad or even a shopping spree. Think of a time when you didn't fully embrace the other person's vision. Without your agreement, how committed were you to the activities or outcomes envisioned by a parent or friend? When visions are simply "laid on our lives," we often respond with far less than wholehearted enthusiasm or efforts.

So, when we ask "Is visioning still relevant?" a part of what we are asking is "Can you imagine being fully committed and giving 100% effort for a vision that you did not help to create?" There have been countless research studies supporting the importance of stakeholder buy-in and support (Donaldson & Preston, 1995; Freeman, 1984; Hultman, Yeboah-Banin, & Formaniuk, 2016; Kee & Newcomer, 2008). In 2019, the research has not shifted; new findings are not suggesting that visioning is any less important today than in the past. Nor do they suggest that stakeholder buy-in is any less essential.

Julie Chakraverty (2018), a prominent contributor for *Forbes* magazine, notes that a recent report from the World Economic Forum found that a "sense of purpose" in their job is the second-most important norm for millennials when selecting a career, the first being income. Today's new teachers will be the majority in education in just a few years. Great teachers are a resource all school leaders work hard to sustain. If your school community doesn't believe in your school's mission, they won't be teaching long at your school. A vision needs to reflect the reality of our future schools. Multiple stakeholders need the opportunity to be involved in defining the core values and vision. Even if what they see isn't their current reality, if new educators believe the school is moving in the right direction, they will stay involved and continue to contribute to the mission. These movers will be the people taking action and making it happen. Teamwork doesn't just matter; shared visions are the key to school success.

Factors to Consider for Visioning at Your School or District

John Medina (2008), molecular biologist, authored a book titled *Brain Rules*, in which he notes that the physical attribute of ocular vision trumps all other senses. Medina notes that vision is not actually done with our eyes; it's a function of our brain. Following a complicated explanation, it's clear that although we consider vision to be a reliable tool, it seldom provides a perfectly accurate representation of our world. Instead, the brain takes in data from the eye, makes an analysis based on other information and environmental factors, and then determines what it thinks is out there. Instead of a snapshot from a camera, we see an interpreted piece of art. It's a prediction based on many optical filters and brain waves. This is similar to the creation of a school-based shared vision. It may not be 100% accurate, but it should be the multiplexing of many voices and ideas, combined with what's right for students. Only then will our shared visions elevate to purpose and belief. This is what binds us, drives us, and keeps a school team moving toward success.

Visioning Onward is the change agent that will take slow, impactful efforts and shift them to a different place. No more will the vision be only a statement on a website or letterhead; instead the vision will have the potential to be the tipping point taking your school over the transformation ledge into progress. A tipping point of a potential change is defined by Gladwell (2000) as a turning point in the journey where little causes have a big effect. He also indicates that to have this type of shift, the need for change must be contagious, and the change takes place in a dramatic moment. That's what we are suggesting here: working to create a shared vision that gains momentum in intense and infectious ways.

One way to begin your visioning is to first reflect on the depth and importance that has been placed on visioning at your school or district.

Key Learning 2.3

History of Visioning at Your School or District

What is the history of visioning at your school or district? Is it authentic in that it reflects the ideas, needs, and desires of key stakeholders? For a good example of authentic visioning, check out the website for the city of Cape Girardeau, Missouri at **Online Resource 2.1**

Could you consider a process similar to the one used in Cape Girardeau that uses an active visioning process with wall charts and markers, the development of team spirit, and using cell phones to capture ideas?

Have you tapped into the power of shared visioning? If so, how?

When you look at your school, what sparks your interest, which elements are unique to the population you serve or the community surrounding you? Is there a contagious element or an exciting point of pride worthy of growing? Does the current vision push the envelope to create a learning environment in which students learn not only knowledge but also skills to be ready for the future? Here are a few questions to help guide your thinking:

- Does your school face any seemingly unsurmountable challenges?

- Has your school undergone dramatic changes in its population base or its designated function and purpose (e.g., has the district redrawn school boundaries, has your school merged with another school, or has it become a center to serve specific district needs)?

- Has your school created a vision for incorporating virtual reality as a primary tool to guide learning?

- When you look at the use of technology in everyday lives, is it incorporated in a similar way in classrooms?

- How is your school addressing balance or the consideration of social-emotional learning or nonacademic factors?

- What do you know about job and career trends? How has this affected your vision?

- When was the last time your teachers developed a vision without being driven by the need to focus on improved academic test scores?

How Do Visions Relate to a School's Purpose?

When considering visioning and options for growth and development, it helps to begin by considering the role of the school. What are the functions of schools? Certainly, furthering student learning and academic achievement are primary, and visions for schools are highly likely to somehow reference these values. However, as the recent movement to ensure that schools are "trauma informed" has documented, other individual and societal needs must be taken into consideration (Dombo & Sabatino, 2019; Overstreet & Chafouleas,

2016; Walkley & Cox, 2013). Schools are inundated with trauma. Before the age of four, one of every four children will have experienced a trauma; by the age of 18, almost 60% will have experienced at least one traumatic event such as sexual assault, physical and emotional violence, or bullying (CDC, 2019a). Further, suicide is the second-leading cause of death for youth ages 10–19 (CDC, 2019b).

When we examine the paths schools have taken, particularly in light of trauma and social emotional needs, it is clear that course corrections are needed. Looking at the history of visioning for improvements in education, it appears that schools, like some businesses, have taken a few missteps along the way to implement changes. It is almost as if they have fallen out of love with visioning. Suzanne Bates (2016), business consultant and author of *All the Leader You Can Be*, believes that many businesses are missing a vision, which prevents employees from realizing they are a part of something bigger. Is your school mission and vision tied to a larger view of the needs of the world? A current, relevant reflection will add to the common understandings of all stakeholders. This realignment of vision will allow resources to flow toward unified goals.

Key Learning 2.4

Inspiration and Dreams

Check to see if this resonates with you: Imagine that you are involved in school or district planning that inspires and frees school teams to innovate, dream, and be responsive to local values, needs, concerns, and opportunities. How might that occur? Although Chapter 3 will give you a more detailed guide, we ask you to begin to consider the possibility that you are involved in a process that inspires teachers.

Visioning and ESSA

We all have visions. Some are more futuristic; others are more limited. Some visions may even take us back a few years, perhaps even back to the pre-No Child Left Behind era. Some of the trends for school visions in the 1990s, for example, focused on direct preparation for employment through career exploration and vocational training. In the 1980s, the focus was on quality. Stimulated by *A Nation at Risk* (The National Commission on Excellence in Education, 1983), a report whose general theme was that the US education system was falling behind other countries and required immediate reform, educators and the general public were reminded that we could not afford to ignore academic excellence.

The vision that emerges from ESSA, in comparison to the No Child Left Behind Act, is one of more local control and less reliance on academic achievement as the sole measure of success. Thankfully, in these past few years there has been a swing back toward more balance, with greater realization of the importance of meaningful learning experiences. Yet, in many places all these changes occurred without local, school-based visioning. Changes cannot just be a reaction—they must be well thought-out plans to prepare students for the demands of our ever-changing world.

In light of all that is happening in schools today, we must consider if schools might need to do more. Perhaps it is John Hattie's *Visible Learning* (2009), Fullan et al.'s *Deep Learning* (2017) George Couros's *Innovator's Mindset* (2015), T. Dintersmith and T. Wagner's *Most Likely to Succeed* (2015), or Daniel A. Domenech, M. Sherman, and J. L. Brown's *Personalizing 21st Century Education* (2016) that inspire you. How could some of these more recent educational trends affect your vision?

What Can We Conclude?   After being touted in the 1990s as an important organizational development tool, visioning seems to have been dismissed at the local level during the last couple of decades. Visioning is no longer prevalent in many, if not most, neighborhood schools, regardless of what occurs at the national level. Or, if it is not dismissed, perhaps it has been replaced with school improvement planning (SIP) and constrained by the expectations for SIP. SIP tends to be more granular, with a focus on specific goals and objectives and development of action and strategic plans. In contrast, visioning is more about looking at the big picture, of dreaming about possibilities. As Beecher and Sweeny (2008) have indicated, the school improvement process begins with analyzing strengths and weaknesses and developing a school mission and strategic plan replete with goals, objectives, and action plans. As their work indicates, schools often bypass visioning exercises by using this process. If we look at state mandates, this is often to expedite the development of a SIP, particularly for schools that are low performing. A quick fix is not the answer.

Commitment Over Compliance

Authors Heifetz and Linsky (2002), cofounders of Cambridge Leadership Associates (CLA), an international leadership development practice that grew out of 30 years of examining and teaching the practice of leadership at Harvard University's John F. Kennedy School of Government, offer yet another insight about vision in their book *Leadership on the Line.* Here's what that contrast between compliance and commitment looks like when we consider the issue of teacher evaluation:

Compliance Model	Commitment Model
The harried leader completes checklists or necessary technological data after one visit to the classroom. She/he then sends the information electronically to the teacher, indicating, "See me if you have a question." This process may happen twice each year, with the teacher knowing ahead of time when the evaluation will occur. Although the compliant leader has followed timelines and completed documents, this model is ineffective in ensuring teacher growth and instructional expertise.	The leader intentionally guards time each day to visit classrooms unannounced for 10 to 15 minutes per room. This leader is committed to a clear purpose: ensuring that every student has an effective teacher in front of him/her every day. Following the visit, the leader and teacher meet briefly in a face-to-face, focused conversation about the visit. The teacher is a partner in the discussion, bringing experience, reasoning, and questions to the table for consideration. This process of observation followed by feedback conversation is completed ideally seven to eight times each year. The result is that committed leaders are focused on growth, frequent feedback, and individualized support and accountability for each teacher. They realize that when we want to support teacher growth, it's our conversations that matter, not our checklists. This model of commitment to excellent evaluation practices goes far beyond compliance and results in a credible system that ensures teacher progress.

Heifetz and Linsky (2002) are so clear in their assertion about the contrast between compliance and commitment that they even indicate *organizations that focus on compliance will never rise above the level of mediocrity. Only organizations that focus on commitment will achieve excellence.* That's a sobering message well worth our consideration!

Uncommon leaders, who encourage and support their organizational vision with enthusiasm, will light a spark of innovation, creativity, and energy in their people! When leaders focus on ownership, the vision is widely owned and shared—the work rests on shared energy and expertise. Leaders who go beyond compliance and model commitment to the vision will lead their organization to surprising new heights and will help their people strive for excellence.

Visioning in Schools—Opportunities Today to Recreate Education

Schools today have an opportunity to recreate themselves—to turn from the automatons that churned out high-achieving students (or attempted to) to schools that will lead children into the future. Schools are no longer in a place where they can focus solely on academic content. Our students need to be prepared for college, careers, and civic life success in this 21st century world that will require skills such as critical thinking, problem-solving, collaboration, and oral communication.

Vision guides leadership. Start the process, and make a path that illuminates the travel for all those who follow. Schools can step up and communicate a far-reaching, future-touching message. These beliefs will create actions that will attract resources, challenges, and the right people to continue the journey (Maxwell, 1999).

Today, changes in many sectors of society are likely to occur at a rapid pace with little time for careful planning and assessment. With outreach and communication at our fingertips, movements can spread like wildfire, growing quickly, with concurrent evaluation, reassessment, and modifications. At the same time, innovations in technology and science in particular are occurring at a pace that demands attention, staying in touch, and keeping up with leaders in particular fields. Schools should be a part of this wave in future forward thinking and implementation.

Where Is Your School (Or District) Headed?

Some schools already have a vision or have adopted the district's vision. If your vision is reflective of a consensus derived from a participatory process involving teachers, staff, students, and community, then congratulations are in order. While at your school, key stakeholders may have been involved in a participatory visioning process. Even then, visions can be limited. For many schools and districts, visioning with a sense of ownership and local buy-in seems to be *limited by the protocol for creating SIPs, the district vision, and the state and federal requirements.*

Visioning From the Field

Many schools and districts appear to be taking advantage of the lull in pushing solely academic achievement to help their staff and students prepare for the future. Following are three examples of innovative visions that have a holistic orientation. Some of the themes from these visions, which are common to other schools and districts in the United States as well, include diversity, integration of technology, and collaborative learning to both support active learning and prepare students for the future.

The El Paso Independent School District (EPISD), serving more than 60,000 students, has fifty-eight elementary schools, ten high schools, and fifteen middle schools and several innovative programs such as a medical magnet high school and an early college high school. EPISD is a high-poverty school district: 70 percent of the students are economically disadvantaged. Diversity is great in EPISD: 83 percent of the students are Hispanic, 10 percent are White, and 4 percent are African American/Black. The vision for EPISD is that EPISD "will be a premier educational institution, source of pride and innovation, and the cornerstone of emerging economic opportunities producing a twenty-first century workforce."

Key components of the EPISD vision statement include the following:

- To become a premier educational institution

- To be a source of pride and innovation

- To be the cornerstone of emerging economic opportunities, producing a 21st century workforce

(Continued)

(Continued)

To achieve this vision, in 2016 a five-year plan was created; strategic priorities included active learning, great community schools, community partnerships, and leading with character and ethics. The El Paso Independent School District 2020 Strategic Plan (see **Online Resource 2.2**) indicated that "as a traditional urban school district, El Paso schools had previously focused primarily on preparing students for Texas assessments." The new leadership team and board of trustees saw the opportunity to focus on broader aims and bigger goals for El Paso's learners' readiness rates by helping EPISD teachers create innovative, active and personalized learning environments that challenge and support all students.

The overarching goals posted on the website include the following:

- All students and staff will participate in active learning and have deeper understanding.
- Families will have options for great schools.
- We will implement tools, resources, and training that support blended and personalized learning for both students and teachers.

The EPISD website presents considerable information in its five-year plan, including student learning goals that focus on helping students become creative thinkers, informed problem solvers, effective bilingual communicators, responsible leaders, productive citizens, and socially and emotionally responsible adults. Their plan is comprehensive, and the district has seen substantial growth since the plan was implemented in 2016.

Compare the EPISD vision to the following two vision statements. Each presents a unique picture of the values of the school or district and its directions for the future.

Visioning From the Field

The vision statement for Park View Elementary in Simi Valley, California is: "Growing, learning, and achieving together."

The vision for Park View Elementary suggests an overarching theme of togetherness with an emphasis on growth, learning, and achievement. Although this seems like a great slogan, it is only when one reads the goals for Park View that one gains a deeper appreciation for Park View's vision. Among the fourteen goals are the following:

- Creating a safe learning environment that empowers students to develop personal responsibility

- Creating a professional learning community where students learn, staff work together to improve student achievement, and efforts are assessed on the basis of results

- Holding high academic and behavioral expectations for *all* students and communicating these expectations to parents and students

- Collaborating within and across grade levels to focus instruction on target subskills needed for growth

- Developing a community of learners that recognize and respect each other's differences and similarities by providing students opportunities to interact with each other in organized instructional activities

(Park View Elementary, n.d.)

What is striking about the "how" as portrayed in Park View's vision and goals is the clarity of the images of actions: creating safe learning environments, empowering students, students and staff learning together, maintaining high expectations, engaging in cross-grade collaboration, and creating a respectful, inclusive community.

Visioning From the Field

Visions for schools vary widely. Examine the vision for Washington County Public Schools (n.d.) in Hagerstown, Maryland: "Washington County Public Schools, in partnership with community members, educates and enables all students to fully access opportunities afforded them in a rapidly changing, diverse, global society." Their website indicates that

through magnet and advanced programs, technical specialties, outdoor experiences, special education, technology and the arts, WCPS prepares students for chosen college or career paths after education. Innovative leadership and programming create an educational experience to ensure that students have the opportunity to succeed in a 21st Century environment.

The video *Building Community* at the Washington County Public Schools website also highlights collaborative learning, innovation, and supports for a diverse community of students (see **Online Resource 2.3**).

Key Learning 2.5

What About Your School?

Look at the three visions for schools, and then examine the vision for your school. Compare the goals for your school, the EPISD, Park View, and Washington County Public Schools. Then compare the vision and goals for Grange Elementary that are presented in the introduction to this book. What can you say about where your school is headed?

Conclusions—Visioning in a Time of Uncertainty and Implications for Schools

One of the fundamental issues of today is that we are in a time in which the future is not certain. Statistics abound about how the changing nature of employment due to technology, globalization, and a myriad of other factors will affect our way of living and working. A recent study titled "The Future of Employment: How Susceptible Are Jobs to Computerisation?" by Dr. Michael Osborne from Oxford University's Department of Engineering Science and Dr. Carl Benedikt Frey of the Oxford Martin School "estimates that 47 percent of jobs in the US are 'at risk' of being automated in the next 20 years" (Frey & Osborne, 2013). Threatening to affect both blue- and white-collar jobs, these trends have serious implications for education leaders and their role in preparing students to be ready for the challenges and opportunities that the future holds for their life and work.

This is not a new problem as throughout history new technologies have changed the way we work and live. Think about the printing press, the telephone, electricity, the automobile, the internet, and the iPhone. What is critical to remember is that these inventions began with an idea, a vision. Margaret Mead said more than 50 years ago, "We must educate our children for what no one knew yesterday and prepare our schools for what no one knows yet." The challenge for education remains with us today.

In Chapter 3, we will share examples of visions and goals from highly successful businesses. If you are looking for additional inspiration and insights into the relevancy of participatory visioning, turn to Chapter 3. In that chapter, we will help you penetrate the layers of reality at your school to deepen your understanding of the potential of your team and your path. However, for now, we leave you with an invitation to continue with your own internal dialogue, perhaps a process of reflection, and some incubation of any of the ideas that you may be considering regarding your school. Could there be something to the wisdom of Tanner Christensen (2015), a product designer at Facebook and author of *The Creativity Challenge?* According to Christensen, "visioning is the most important part of the learning process" (Bryant & Stratton College, 2016).

We realize that visioning, to be effective, takes time. In fact, we would argue that one-shot visioning is comparable to drive-by professional development. Visions are not created in 30-minute staff meetings. Rather, robust visions take time. CEI developed its vision for Heart Centered Learning™ over several years, revisiting themes and concepts with a core team of educational leaders on multiple occasions. As Aaron Brengard found, the vision for his school was developed with thoughtful discussions with staff and community and reflection over several months. The question we leave you with is this: "Can we really afford not to take this time?"

Practical Points to Ponder

- Vision drives change. Shared vision drives transformation and excellence. What changes might you or a group of key leaders in your school want to drive?

- When you consider the history of your school and the commitment of the teachers, what might help further visioning? Where is there agreement and coherence?

- What barriers might you face as you move forward with visioning?

As we've learned in this chapter, a vision sparks possibility and inspires action. Involve your community members and stakeholders from the beginning to get a rich blend of ideas and perspectives and to ensure buy-in and success. Keep your vision clear, concise, and captivating. Taking the time to work together and develop this vision will serve you well. You will grapple with the possibilities, prioritize your terms, and define your ideal. Everyone will know where you're heading and how you plan to get there. What if everyone around you is inspired, engaged, and empowered? What if your community was unified behind a common vision? What if you believed that together you can achieve the improbable?

Ideas for Leading and Learning

- An effective vision allows us to see what's ahead and where we need to travel as an organization. For your school family, what are the three core beliefs held about students, learning, and the school community?

- Consider visioning from the perspective of another leader or staff member in your school. What would you expect them to agree on in your framework of vision, and what would you anticipate them disagreeing with?

- In our approach to visioning, we suggest considering voices and input that travel in our pipeline to create a strong outcome. Who among your school stakeholders influences the direction you head? Whose voice needs to be elevated to a higher level? Who needs to listen?

- Consider the world your students are preparing for, not the world you were prepared in. Does your vision include how and where they are learning? What will be different? What do your students need? How will this be part of your vision for change?

Resources to Explore

Scan the QR Code or visit https://resources.corwin.com/visioningonward to access live links to these videos and other resources.

Online Resource 2.4 Video: Peter Senge—Shared Vision
Online Resource 2.5 Video: Simon Sinek—Finding Your Vision
Online Resource 2.6 Video: Katie Martin—Teachers Create What They Experience

Online Resource 2.7 Video: World Economic Forum—The New Vision for Education
Online Resource 2.8 Video: The Center Online—Did You Know, in 2028 . . .
Online Resource 2.9 Video: John Hattie—Why Are So Many of Our Teachers and Schools So Successful?
Online Resource 2.10 Video: Todd Rose—The Myth of Average
Online Resource 2.11 Article: ISTE—8 Ways to Establish Shared Vision
Online Resource 2.12 Article: John G. Gabriel and Paul C. Farmer—How to Help Your School Thrive Without Breaking the Bank
Online Resource 2.13 TopNonprofits—30 Examples of Nonprofit Vision Statements
Online Resource 2.14 NASSP and NAESP—Leadership Matters: What the Research Says About the Importance of Principal Leadership

Chapter 3

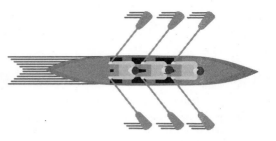

21ST CENTURY CONCERNS—FOOD FOR THOUGHT

> To be successful today, we must cope with a flood of knowledge and data about the present; we must also be able to anticipate the future. . . . The world today is a moving target.
>
> —*Leonard Mlodinow (2018, p. 219)*

Before we take you further down the path to visioning, we would like to guide you through some what-if scenarios. This chapter is designed to help you consider not only what might be for your school but also how you can learn from some pretty amazing entrepreneurs who have changed our lives and are continuing to change our daily routines.

Dreams, Visioning Onward, and Changes in Schools

What is a vision? The University of Kansas Center for Community Health and Development (n.d.) puts it this way: "Your vision is your dream. It's what your organization believes are the ideal conditions for your community; that is, how things would look if the issue important to you were completely, perfectly addressed."

For additional guidance on this topic, see Jenette Nagy and Stephen B. Fawcett's 2018 article, "Proclaiming Your Dream:

Developing Vision and Mission Statements." You can find a live link to the article at **Online Resource 3.1**. One of the things we like about the University of Kansas Center for Community Health and Development definition is that it considers *your community*, implying that visions may differ according to local circumstances and needs.

Peter Senge and colleagues (2012) write that

learning is driven by vision. Too many organizations, including schools, ignore this precept. . . . Some may fear that allowing students—or teachers for that matter—to pursue their 'vision' in schools means letting people do whatever they want, abandoning rigor, and lowering educational standards. Nothing could be further from the truth.

(p. 27)

Before beginning to formulate a vision for your community, we suggest you consider advice from a few thought leaders of our era. When describing the importance of technology for the future of education, Michael Fullan (2012) in his book *Stratosphere: Integrating Technology, Pedagogy, and Change Knowledge* states that technology should meet four criteria, being "i) irresistibly engaging (for students and teachers); ii) elegantly efficient and easy to use; (iii) technologically ubiquitous 24/7; and (iv) steeped in real-life problem solving" (p. 4). Fullan believes that there "will be a great appetite for the new way" and that the pedagogy should be based on "partnering with students." It is interesting that in an article comparing 3-D printers for the International Society for Technology in Education (ISTE), Trevor Takayama (2018), a technology teacher at Amherst-Pelham Regional Public Schools in Massachusetts, mentions two challenges that might be applicable to many innovations: costs/funding and the learning curve. Our question, given these statements, is will our appetite be great enough to help us overcome the challenges? Or will we be complacent or perhaps remain more interested in meeting our immediate needs?

In considering visions, it is important to reflect on both the challenges we are facing today and the dilemma of how to adapt to what is to come. In his latest book, Leonard Mlodinow, a theoretical physicist, describes the need for flexible or *elastic* thinking to help us adjust to the new circumstances that arise. Some of the skills that Mlodinow (2018) highlights that are needed to cope include: the ability to let go of things that are comfortable to us, the ability to live with the uncertainty of change, and a willingness to experiment. When we consider visions, what should we do with the challenges that emerge? We will address these in Chapter 7.

Key Learning 3.1

The Future—The Need to Adapt

- As we look to the future, what do you consider to be some of the foremost challenges that schools, teachers, and students are facing?

- Are there specific skills and knowledge that will be needed to further this ability to adapt?

- Is there a possibility that your vision for the future of your schools might address these challenges? How?

In *Back to the Whole*, Nel Noddings (2015) argues that schools need to do more than teach academic skills—a more holistic view is needed. She argues six other aims must be integrated into our curricula and instruction including *health, vocation, citizenship, worthy family membership, worthy use of leisure, and ethical character.*

The vision of the Ashoka Changemaker Schools is to establish schools where empathy is the foundation for "solutions that are guided by humility, understanding, and compassion." Ashoka, with its *empathy changemaker* schools, is a private organization that has 260 changemaker schools around the world, with 89 in the United States. They believe

> empathy is the foundation for children to live successful lives and create change in the world. Change is essential in today's society. . . . To thrive as individuals and a society, everyone must be a changemaker, able to take initiative to positively contribute in a world of uncertain rules, fluid institutions, and constant change.
>
> (Ashoka Foundation, n.d.)

Ashoka's vision serves as a common thread among changemaker schools: "A shared vision of schools as sites of social change and a belief that students and educators have a role in shaping the system itself" (Ashoka Foundation, 2017, p. 23). They share a common belief that "innovative practices and a culture of love, empathy, and collaboration in our schools can shape a generation of changemakers" (p. 29). Components of their vision include things such as cultivating mutual trust, elevating student voices, and teaching relevant curriculum. However, the foundation is *empathy*, which is not considered an add-on but a requisite for "solutions that are guided by humility, understanding, and compassion" (p. 65). Ashoka (2016), in its recent book *Changemakers: Educating With Purpose*, provides several examples of how a focus on empathy has led to increased academic achievement. You can access the free tool kit by visiting **Online Resource 3.2.**

Key Learning 3.2

Your Exquisite Dream for Your School or District

1. What is your dream for your school? Is it a no-holds-barred dream?

2. Check all that apply, and make notes next to each item. Is your dream for your school:

   □ Irresistibly engaging?

   □ Elegantly efficient?

   □ Ubiquitous? Does it permeate your school/district?

   □ Steeped in or applicable to real-life problem solving?

3. Does your vision . . .

   □ Integrate aims for health, vocation, citizenship, worthy family membership, worthy use of leisure, and ethical character?

   □ Incorporate anything related to developing empathy or compassion?

   □ Consider a need for rigor?

4. We will take you through a more in-depth visioning process in Chapter 4; however, for now, examine your dream. What would change at your school or district if your dream was implemented?

5. What difference could your dream make?

6. If you have a vision statement for your school, examine the current statement, and compare it to your dream.

Do Visions Make a Difference?

Let us turn for a minute to the business world. Businesses today are continuing to develop shared visions. ChangeFactory, an Australian consulting company that specializes in change management and business transformation, reminds us that shared vision statements

> should be a means by which we describe a desired outcome that invokes a vivid mental picture of our goal. As leaders, a vision statement should inspire and energise us, our subordinates, our colleagues and our other stakeholders. . . . A vision statement should say something about us, our organisation, our operating environment, our dream. When we read it, it should tell us where we are going. We should not be able to substitute our vision statement for other organisations inside and outside our industry.
>
> > (ChangeFactory, n.d.)

To hear a podcast of Kevin Dwyer, Managing Director of ChangeFactory, talking about values, vision, and mission statements, visit **Online Resource 3.3.**

They suggest that a shared vision statement should meet the following criteria:

✓ Short and to the point

✓ Broad and encompassing of the entire organization

✓ Written in the present, not future tense—it describes what we will feel, hear, think, say, and do as if we had reached our vision now

✓ Written using unequivocal language—it does not use business speak, words like *maximize* or *minimize*, or include numeric measures of success

✓ Positive, not a description of what is not wanted—people are motivated by positive pictures, not by negative ones

✓ A vision that people buy into, hold in their minds, can see and feel, and aspire to achieve because of its power, effect, and reward

✓ A tool to build an inspirational and motivational picture, the same picture, in people's minds

✓ Developed through collaborative participation, not dropped on the organization by the leader.

Strategic Business Leader (2008) recommends starting the visioning process by asking, "What is, and more importantly will be, the essence of the business five years from now if we are extraordinarily successful?" For additional guidance from Strategic Business Leader on developing a shared vision visit **Online Resource 3.4.**

Five Great Companies

To help reinforce the power of visioning, in the next few pages we will review the role of visioning in the history and growth of five major companies: Amazon, Starbucks, Accenture, Apple, and Microsoft. As you review this information, consider advice from the ChangeFactory (2014) article, "The Components of a Good Vision Statement," which can be accessed from **Online Resource 3.5.**

Learning From Five Giants

As you read through each of these scenarios, consider the following:

- The possible takeaways for education and your school or district
- Anything that you might be able to replicate or build upon

Amazon

"Our vision is to be earth's most customer centric company; to build a place where people can come to find and discover anything they might want to buy online."

The elements of the Amazon vision include the following:

- Be the foremost global customer-centric company (responding to needs of customers)
- Build a place where customers can find and discover anything they want to buy online

Jeff Bezos, founder of Amazon, transformed Amazon from being a small online retailer based in his garage to a worldwide iconic example of a successfully run electronic commerce platform. Although the company was based in Bezos's garage, it managed to sell books in 45 different countries during its first month. By 1996, only two years after its launch, Amazon had reached a total of 180,000 customer accounts. Two years later, Amazon went international with online booksellers in Germany and the United Kingdom. Bezos earned recognition all over the world. In 1999, he was honored by *Time* magazine as person of the year. According to Amazon (2019), "Over the last 5 years, Amazon has created more than 125 jobs in the US every day."

Starbucks

Some companies, such as Starbucks, combine their mission and vision statements. In 2008, Starbucks' vision was "to establish Starbucks as the most recognized and respected brand in the world and become a national company with values and guiding principles that employees could be proud of" (Farfan, 2017).

Ever since, Howard Schultz has worked tirelessly to realize Starbucks' mission through the lens of humanity by upholding the company's values of "creating a culture of warmth and belonging where everyone is welcome, acting with courage, being present, and connecting with transparency, dignity and respect" (Farfan, 2017). In 2017, Starbucks' vision statement was "to inspire and nurture the human spirit – one person, one cup and one neighborhood at a time" (Farfan, 2017).

Abhijeet Pratap (2019) in a web log post describes the inspirational aspects of the Starbucks' mission and vision statement:

> It definitely reflects the special focus of Starbucks on the customer. There are two things that are notable about Starbucks' mission statement. The first is the human spirit. The second is the oneness—one cup, one person, one neighborhood. Seen from an analytical angle there are several things missing from this statement whether we consider it a mission or a vision. It does not spell out its market, its customers, or even its employees. It highlights none of those aspects of business. It spells out more like a philosophy at whose center is each customer. Inspiring and nurturing the human spirit.

How did Starbucks' vision originate, and how did its founder, Howard Schultz, go on to "establish Starbucks as the premier purveyor of the finest coffee in the world while maintaining our uncompromising principles while we grow" (Farfan, 2017)? Starbucks' extraordinary story began in 1971 when three former students from the University of San Francisco, Jerry Baldwin, Zev Siegl, and Gordon Bowker, opened up the first Starbucks store in Seattle's Pike Place Market. They named their store after the first mate in Herman Melville's *Moby Dick*, which they felt "evoked the romance of the high seas and the seafaring tradition of the early coffee traders" (Starbucks, n.d.). Their original plan was to sell high-quality coffee beans along with roasting equipment.

In 1982, Schultz earned his position as Starbucks' director of retail operations and marketing. After taking an eye-opening trip to Milan, Schultz convinced the founders of Starbucks to open their first coffeehouse in downtown Seattle. Meanwhile, Schultz established his own coffee shop—Il Giornale. A couple years later, Schultz purchased Starbucks and changed Il Giornale's name to Starbucks Corporation with the help of local investors.

By 1989, Schultz had founded a total of fifty-five Starbucks stores. In 1996, Starbucks went international by opening a store in Japan—Starbucks' first store outside of North America. Having grown up in a public housing project in Brooklyn, New York, Schultz felt a responsibility to implement social programs in an attempt to extend help to the community. Consequently, he has created programs such as The Starbucks Foundation and Partner Match and Community Service Grants. These programs, along with several others, donate money to nonprofit organizations around the world and fund community-building programs. Starbucks also provides its employees, which are considered its partners, with the Starbucks College Achievement Plan, offering full tuition coverage and benefits through Arizona State University. From an environmental stance, Starbucks has continually contributed to improving biodiversity conservation, providing education and agricultural training and increasing levels of water sanitation. Through its partnership with Ethos Water, Starbucks raises awareness about water conservation and provides impoverished children with access to clean water. Deservedly, Starbucks has been commended for its efforts by the Ethisphere Institute for twelve years in a row being titled one of the World's Most Ethical Companies.

As is stated in Starbucks' Company Profile, "At Starbucks, we have always believed in the importance of building a great, enduring company, that strikes a balance between profitability and social conscience" (Starbucks, n.d.).

Accenture

Accenture, a Fortune 500 and leading global professional services company, describes its vision this way:

> The real world is coming online, as smart objects, devices, and machines increase our insight into control over the physical world. . . . Picture a workforce that extends beyond your employees—one that consists of any user connected to the internet. Cloud, social, and collaboration technologies now allow organizations to tap into vast pools of human resources.
>
> (Accenture, 2016, p.15)

In 2019, Accenture now describes its vision for the post-digital world:

What will this post-digital era look like?

A world where individualization and instant on-demand capabilities will make it possible for businesses to capture and deliver on momentary markets.

The next wave of technology will make it possible for products, services and even people's surroundings to be deeply customized—or what Accenture is calling "individualization"—and delivered instantly on demand (Daugherty, 2019).

In 2016, Accenture described its *vision of people and cultures that must become more digital* and how technology plays a disruptive role in helping "human workers work humanly better." (Accenture, 2016).

In 2001, Accenture, one of the world's leading consulting companies, emerged from what began in 1989 as the business division of an accounting organization— Arthur Andersen (Accenture, 2000). Years later, Accenture prides itself in solving its "clients' toughest challenges by providing unmatched services in strategy, consulting, digital technology, and operations" (Accenture, n.d.). With clients in more than 120 countries and sixteen consecutive appearances in *Fortune's* "World's Most Admired Companies" list, Accenture has proven to be perhaps one of the most outstanding success stories of all time.

Accenture's astonishing success story begins before it was given its current name. In 1951, Joseph Glickauf revealed his innovative Glickiac computer, and within a few years it was installed at GE Appliance Park for commercial use. By 1972, Glickauf's firm developed its first computerized dictionary: Lexicon (Accenture 2018).

In 2007, with revenue of $16.6 billion, *DiversityInc* named Accenture one of the "Top 50 Companies for Diversity" (Accenture, 2018). A year later, Accenture earned a place in Ethisphere Institute's "World's Most Ethical Companies" list (Accenture, 2018). Accenture continues to be a model of success on a day-to-day basis.

Apple

Apple has been transformative in many ways. They completely revolutionized the music and mobile phone industries. They've transformed how we communicate, get around, and interact with our environment. From the iPod, iPhone, Apple Watch, iTunes, and the App Store, they've fundamentally changed our daily lives. Apple capitalized on the so-called Fourth Industrial Revolution, defined by vast increases in computer processor power, storage capacity, and internet connectivity (Schwab, 2017). They have disrupted industries with simple, delightful, and intuitive products, but it's their ability to continuously refine their products that keeps them on top.

Apple's vision statement is:

> We believe that we are on the face of the earth to make great products and that's not changing. We are constantly focusing on innovating. We believe in the simple not the complex. We believe that we need to own and control the primary technologies behind the products that we make, and participate only in markets where we can make a significant contribution. We believe in saying no to thousands of projects, so that we can really focus on the few that are truly important and meaningful to us. We believe in deep collaboration and cross-pollination of our groups, which allow us to innovate in a way that others cannot. And frankly, we don't settle for anything less than excellence in every group in the company, and we have the self-honesty to admit when we're wrong and the courage to change.

(Cook, 2009)

They focus on innovation and simplicity. Instead of trying to do many things adequately, they focus on doing a few things remarkably. Their vision statement is lofty and inspiring, yet it provides clear guidance, values, and structure to spur action. The vision statement reminds employees and stakeholders to strive for innovation, simplicity, strategic focus, deep collaboration, honesty, and courage in their everyday decisions, tasks, and interactions.

Microsoft

Bill Gates and Paul Allen founded Microsoft in 1975 to produce software for the Altair 8800, an early personal computer. Within three years, their sales topped $1 million. Microsoft has remained at the top of the computing and technology industry for more than thirty years. It has continued its success during times of incredible technological transformation, which usually leaves companies vulnerable to being knocked off by disruptive technologies (Silverthorne, 2002). Microsoft has been able to read and react to technological trends with impressive efficiency by creating elaborate internal processes and structures. The Microsoft vision statement affirms:

> Global diversity and inclusion is an integral and inherent part of our culture, fueling our business growth while allowing us to attract, develop and retain this best talent, to be more innovative in the products and services we develop, in the way we solve problems, and in the way we serve the needs of an increasingly global and diverse customer and partner base.
>
> (Microsoft, n.d.)

The elements of the Microsoft vision include the following:

- Be a place that embraces global diversity and inclusion
- Stimulate business growth while recruiting, developing, and retaining talented employees
- Increase product and service innovations
- Expand ways of problem solving
- Expand global and diverse customer and partner base

In its mission statement, Microsoft focuses on people—the employees, customers, and partners who enable the company to be successful. It focuses on hiring, developing, and retaining the right talent because the employees are the lifeblood of the company. It values inclusivity, innovation, and collaborative problem-solving, relying on these strengths to help it remain competitive in an increasingly globalized and diverse world.

Comparing Visions

Each of these vision statements from these highly successful companies presented an easily identifiable statement that served as a basis for helping the company to stay on track as it grew. The visions helped the companies to be forward thinking, to connect with customers, and to develop a distinct brand.

Table 3.1 provides a side-by-side analysis of some of the key components of these visions.

Visions as Disruptions

Jay Samit is a Hollywood tech executive who has developed technology for Apple, Microsoft, and Intel. In his book *Disrupt You!*, Samit (2015) argues, "Disruptors don't have to discover something new; they just have to discover a practical use for new discoveries" (p. 135).

Heather Simmons (2015) is a former executive and the author of the book *Reinventing Dell*, which looks at the rise and fall of Dell through the 1990s and early 2000s and examines what decision-making strategies did and didn't work for them. In this book, she writes, "Those who disrupt their industries change consumer behavior, alter economics, and transform lives" (p. i). How often have you streamed a new tune off of Apple Music or another streaming service like Spotify or Pandora?

When was the last time you purchased the CD of a new album? CDs and tapes are relics of decades past; vinyl only hangs on for sheer nostalgia.

Table 3.1   Vision Analysis of Five Wildly Successful Industrial Giants

	Amazon	Starbucks	Accenture	Microsoft	Apple
Present tense	Our vision is	Breaks rule—*to establish, to become*	Cloud, social, and collaboration technologies *now allow* organizations to tap into . . . (2016)	Breaks rule—*to be more innovative*	Are [here] *to make great products*
Inspirational phrase	The earth's most customer-centric company	As the most respected brand (original); the world's finest coffee (2015)	Increase our insight over control of our physical world	Attracting and developing the best talent [to increase customer and partner base]	Constantly innovating, focus on the few that are truly important—"On the face of the earth to make great products"
Vivid picture	To find and discover anything they want online	One person, one cup, one neighborhood at a time	Smart objects, devices, machines, a workforce of any internet user	Global diversity and inclusion are integral [to expansion]	Believe in deep collaboration and cross pollination
Evokes emotion	A feeling of satisfaction	That employees can be proud of (original); to inspire and nurture the human spirit (2015)	Access to a vast pool of human resources, picture a workforce that extends beyond your employees	Growth, focus on people even with technology, solving problems—in a way a go-to resource	Believe in simple, not complex solutions; constantly innovating, deep collaboration

Talk about disruptive. But even as physical media sales have plummeted, people have been listening to more music than ever.

How did music come to pervade our lives, and why did we shift from listening through an entire physical album to digitally streaming single tracks by countless artists? With the iPod and the iTunes Store, Apple created a demand for digital music that is now being addressed by five separate streaming services with more than 40 million users each.

Visions, Missions, and Successful Ventures

Apple's successful disruption of the music industry relied on a three-step process: identification, setup, and payoff. First, they saw people burning CDs and downloading digital music files and identified a service Apple could provide. Second, Apple paved the way in October of 2001 with their own platform for digital music—the original iPod. Finally, Apple expanded their own market in 2003 with a way to get more music onto that platform—the iTunes Music Store app for both Mac and Windows.

Apple's current vision statement, released by CEO Tim Cook (2009), paints a broad portrait of Apple's goals. According to Cook, "We believe that we are on the face of the earth to make great products and that's not changing. . . . We believe in the simple not the complex." The company's mission statement is more concrete and lists specific products and innovations by name: "Apple leads the digital music revolution with its iPods and iTunes online store."

Apple's vision statement gives the company an idea of where they want to go; their mission statement fills in the road map of how they get there. What better guidelines could you need if you wanted to reach your goal?

How Innovations Have Disrupted Our Lives

Have you ever altered your routine to stop at Starbucks to grab coffee on your way to work? If not Starbucks, perhaps you stop at a boutique coffee shop. I recently indulged in a Jamaican blueberry coffee from the Amazon at Caffe Amouri, a local coffee shop in our small town. How to describe the coffee? Certainly there's a hint of blueberries, but with the underlying essence of deep, rich caffeine, a hint of lemon and vanilla, and perhaps just a touch of chocolate.

Or do you own a Keurig single-serving coffee maker? We finally broke down and purchased our dream machine—with coffee that is almost as good as the cup of joe that I get at the local caffeine distributors.

Talk about disruptive. However, coffee is now more than a morning cup. It is an experience.

How did our quest for the perfect cup of coffee come about, and why did we shift from coffee with our Mr. Coffee maker in our kitchen to create a demand that is being addressed by more than 28,000 Starbucks around the world, not to mention the hundreds of coffee shops that are now competing for our attention and loyalty?

Visioning—Various Lenses

There are myriad ways to look at visioning. A traditional view would suggest that the process includes representatives from important stakeholder groups, that it begins with an assessment of the status quo, and is developed through a consensus process (Kotter, 1995, p. 3). Many of us are familiar with this process. We begin by deciding who to invite to the table, we consider the current strengths and weaknesses, and we consider some process for coming to an agreement concerning the future. If you examine the history of your school, you even find notes on what happened at the last visioning session.

However, although the process may be similar for urban, rural, and suburban schools, for schools in the Northeast and those in the Southwest, subtle differences in approach may be warranted. As Gregory Cajete, a Tewa from the Santa Clara Pueblo in New Mexico, professor, and director of Native American Studies at the University of New Mexico, indicates in his discussion of tribal education, it is important that visions be inclusive and that they be locally driven. Specific subcultures may find that certain components are more critical for their schools (Cajete, 1994). Cajete, in considering a process for indigenous cultures emphasizes the following:

- Visions are about holistic understanding of important knowledge and not about isolated components.

- Organizational visions are derived from group, not individual, efforts.

- Visions reflect both the knowledge and the values of the group members.

- Visions incorporate many perspectives (positive or negative, happy or frightening, heroic or sad).

Holistic Understanding

There are several implications for schools. Begin by imagining you are opening a shop or a restaurant. It could be a donut shop, a vegetarian restaurant, or perhaps even a used book store. It would be one thing to imagine the food or the products you are selling but another to create an image of the environment—the atmosphere, the clientele, the location, the staffing, and even the interactions you have with customers. *With a holistic vision we try to create vivid images of the sights, smells, sounds, and even kinesthetic experiences. With a holistic vision we consider a multitude of components.*

For your school, perhaps you have a dream of improved technology. It would be one thing to envision virtual reality and holographic images projected on classroom walls. It would be another to create images of how and when this technology is used and images of the classrooms, the teachers, and the students using the technology.

Group Effort

Take your vision for the shop or restaurant you might create or for the use of technology in your school. Imagine implementation if you alone created this vision, and compare what might happen if you had the support of others in your community. Consider the task before you have "realized the vision." Certainly, when a larger group is involved, there are more workers to complete tasks, more people to invest in the vision, and a greater likelihood of obtaining the resources needed to implement the vision.

An additional bonus of group visioning is that others may consider elements that you alone overlooked. Perhaps they can envision a donut shop that includes special packaging for birthday and holiday donuts. Or they envision a vegetarian restaurant that also serves gourmet coffee and has a book-lending library. For your school, when you explore the vision for using technology with a larger group of teachers, perhaps someone will suggest technology Wednesdays during which local community leaders bring innovations such as artificial intelligence to your classrooms either through actual or virtual experiences. Of course, the downside to groupthink is that sometimes really great ideas are watered down. Sometimes when groups come together to envision the future, different visions result in disagreements that are hard to resolve. The process we will take you through in Chapter 4 includes some safeguards to help minimize the downside of our proposed group process.

Knowledge and Values

Let's say your heart is set on the donut shop, yet you know that your passion for donuts is at odds with your goals of fitness and a healthy lifestyle. Or that your vision for using technology may mean that students spend more time interacting with machines and less time interacting with peers. Yet, you know that technology is the path to the future and that 21st century jobs are dependent on technology. You want to assure your students that they are prepared for these jobs—what do you do?

One of the strongest moves is to consider the contradictions that are apparent with these visions. After doing this, you might end up opening a vegetarian restaurant that serves the most wonderful low-fat, healthy donut. Now, perhaps that is something that might happen in a sci-fi alternative reality—or in New York City; for example, donuts made with coconut, almond flour, and mashed bananas; or baked donuts with pumpkin or protein powder and apple cider; or even baked donuts with peanut butter or a cashew nut glaze. Healthier donuts are possible, although they may not meet everyone's expectations; however they may better support your values (healthy, nutritious eating, having fun, breaking a few rules occasionally, and really enjoying life). With technology in school, when you reconsider possibilities that match your values and knowledge, perhaps you will find ways to increase peer interactions as peers share exercises and experiences that involve technology.

Visions That Incorporate Many Perspectives

What do you know about Native American vision quests? In Carlos Castaneda's apprenticeship to Don Juan Matus, he goes into a desert alone and is taken, with the aid of medicinal herbs, through a series of trials and tribulations. He suffers dehydration and experiences nightmares, visitations, and horrifying near-death encounters with ghosts and ancestors from his past. Cajete describes similar experiences as he discusses visioning as a process to gain knowledge from deep within oneself and the natural world (Castaneda, 2016).

While a forty-day vision quest is not for everyone, we do believe that there are lessons that we can learn by looking through a lens that differs from our everyday experiences and perceptions. As a group, we bring a variety of experiences to our visioning processes. As principal Aaron Brengard suggests, seeing a vision through to its implementation is not an easy task. There will be good times and bad, times when the community remains strong in its supports, and times when schools undergo considerable change and the school leader may feel the angst of problem-solving one more time as the inevitable happens.

For our donut shop, it could be that the recipe is amazing, but the ingredients are costly, and the time and labor involved in preparing the donuts is intensive. For the vegetarian restaurant, you may find that your community response fluctuates with the daily specials and that it takes a while to find out which specials are truly magnets that draw in your local diners. With technology implementation in your school, you may find that some technology is more durable than others, that some technology is in higher demand, and that scheduling is, in essence, a nightmare. In each of these instances, more preparation during the visioning stage may have helped prepare you for the inevitable challenges that arise in implementation.

When Cajete suggests that we examine the positive and the negative, the happy and the frightening, and the heroic and the sad, what he is saying is that we need to look at all parts of the elephant because, if one of us only considers the tail and the other only considers the leg, we'll have different visions of the same animal. Ground your visions with a healthy dose of reality and deep thought rather than pie-in-the-sky idealism. This may mean more thorough investigation up front, or it might involve tapping the resources of experts who will help you consider the many sides to your innovation equation.

As you vision, you may wish to consider the implications not only for students but also the key implementers, asking questions such as these:

- How relevant is this for me (us)?

- What are the implications or consequences of this vision for me (us)?

- How well can I (we) cope with or adjust to the consequences of the implementation?

Although answers to these questions should not block a vision or the visioning process, before engaging in a visioning process, it will behoove leaders to consider both the intended and unintended consequences. These questions should be asked repeatedly during the visioning process. For example, if schools have a vision of becoming more compassionate, this could imply a need for professional development, a change in discipline policies and practices, and perhaps even infusing understanding of compassionate practices into the academic curriculum. For implementation to occur, time and resources will need to be devoted to these activities. To find the time, schools may need to change priorities and eliminate segments of previously approved curriculum. Today, as schools are becoming trauma-informed, they are also seeking more counselors and expanding screenings for things such as mental health concerns. This has implications for budgeting and resource allocation as well.

Key Learning 3.3

Looking at Your Dreams More Closely

Earlier in this chapter, we asked questions about your vision for your school. What do you know about the views of others in your school? Do they have the same or a similar vision? Have you had discussions with others about your ideas? What reception are you getting? What concerns, if any, are being expressed? Looking at the criteria from Scherer, consider the following:

- **How relevant is this for me (us)?** Is your vision something that will affect the entire school, or is it more focused on specific grade levels or activities?

- **What are the implications or consequences of this vision for me (us)?** What are the intended and unintended consequences? Will there be changes in curriculum, discipline policies, and time and resource allocation? What will need to shift, and where will the time be gained to implement the vision?

- **How well can I (we) cope with or adjust to the consequences of the implementation?** What can be done to help those who may have difficulty with the new procedures?

Visioning Is Not Missioning

Gabriel and Farmer (2009) in their book *Helping Your School Thrive: Without Breaking the Bank* state:

> Developing strong vision and mission statements can help stakeholders in your school reach such a common understanding. A vision is your school's goal—where you hope to see it in the future. The mission provides an overview of the steps planned to achieve that future. A vision is concise and easy to recall, whereas a mission is lengthier and more explanatory in nature. Your school may also want to establish targets along the way to measure progress toward its vision. . . . You need to know where you want to be before you can determine how you plan to get there.
>
> (p. 45)

Visioning Onward for School Improvement

Peter Senge writes,

> Learning is driven by vision. Too many organizations, including schools, ignore this precept. . . . Some may fear that allowing students—or teachers for that matter—to pursue their "vision" in schools means letting people do whatever they want, abandoning rigor and lowering educational standards. Nothing could be further from the truth.
>
> (Senge et al., 2012, p. 27)

In a longitudinal study of 390 Chicago schools with more than 100,000 responses from teachers, administrators, and students, Bryk, Sebring, Allensworth, Easton, and Luppescu (2010) identified five factors that predicted the greatest success:

- Effective school leadership
- Rigorous instruction
- Collaborative teachers

- Supportive environment

- Strong family–community ties

According to a review of school improvement in Chicago (Bryk et al., 2010), important components for schools are instructional guidance, leadership, professional capacity, learning climate, and parent–community relations. Bryk and colleagues report that when schools demonstrated strengths in at least three of these areas, they were then ten times more likely to show sustained improvement than schools that demonstrated weaknesses in at least three areas. Bryk et al. (2010) also found that "relational trust" was essential and had a "strong reciprocal relationship with the other elements." In a companion brief, *Visioning for School Improvement*, referring to Bryk's work, the New York City Department of Education (n.d.) concluded: "Schools that continuously improve do two things well: they explore new strategies, welcome mistakes as learning opportunities, and they integrate new approaches within the ongoing work of their school, honoring and building from prior work" (p. 2).

Key Learning 3.4

Reflections for Visioning

Look again at the list of factors for success for a shared vision. How important are these factors for the success of your dream? What role do each of them play? Which factors are in place, and which need to be developed?

If your school is one in which teachers have felt punished for low student test scores, you may find a need to debrief. Listen to teachers as they vent before you hop onto some bandwagon for a future initiative. If you have a vision at your school, what does your vision tell you about your school's path? Does the vision feel up-to-date and relevant? Is it challenging and ambitious? Or is it safe? Does it appear to have been overly influenced by test scores or federal and state expectations? What do you know about the past process for visioning at your school? Who was involved? How was it received? And how has your school's vision guided you recently? Can any planned activities be linked to your current vision?

Dreams, Visioning Onward, and Changes in Schools

Of course, for visions to be effective, they must be implemented, and that takes an effective change strategy. As you vision, it might help to be aware of the strategies you will need to move ahead with the actual implementation of the vision. Leithwood, Seashore, Anderson, and Wahlstrom (2004), in synthesizing results of studies of principal leadership, found that three components were necessary for effective change strategies:

- Developing a shared vision, group goals, and high expectations

- Developing and supporting people (teachers, administrators, staff)

- Redesigning the organization with community and parental support and involvement

Conclusions—Collectively Visioning Outside the Box

The process of visioning begins with some ideas of what could be, unrestricted by limitations of time, budget, or resources. Leaders can consider questions about the relevance, commitment, and consequences of the vision. As leaders converse with a small group of colleagues, they can begin to consider the pros and cons from various perspectives. All of this effort serves as a precursor to the more formal visioning process.

Practical Points to Ponder

- Dreams drive visions. How can your school emulate change-making companies that disrupted their industries to change the way we consume coffee, music, and technology-based services?

(Continued)

(Continued)

What seemingly impossible things do you want your school to achieve?

- Visions based on dreams need to remain grounded. How can your school craft a vision that is succinct, inclusive, positive, and inspirational? Is your vision forward-thinking but grounded in the present?

- Are you listening to all the voices in your school or district to figure out how to resolve disagreements so that your vision remains focused *and* all voices are represented? What compromises will you have to make? What concessions will other stakeholders have to make, and how can you justify them for the greater good?

This chapter taught us that successful companies aren't built alone. Many people come together with similar but slightly different visions to create a shared mission statement that clearly defines goals and the path to reach those goals. Another common thread among the visions of the companies we discussed in this chapter is their unrelenting drive to disrupt their industries. They made a space for themselves where there was none before. We challenge you to dream big, but ensure that the journey to your dreams is feasible.

Ideas for Leading and Learning

- We presented several examples of companies that many people viewed as foolish or irrelevant at their inception; yet the founders persisted and made their visions a reality. Which aspects of your vision might be the most difficult for stakeholders in your community to support? How can you convince them that your forward-thinking vision addresses the needs of today and tomorrow?

- For your vision to be successful in your school or district, you can't be the only leader championing it. How many principals in your district or leaders in your school would agree with the areas you've identified as needing the most immediate attention? Is there anyone who might have other ideas for areas of greatest need? How can you merge these viewpoints?

- We often forget to consider consequences of positive change. Bike shares make cities more carbon neutral and citizens healthier, but small bike shops' business suffers. What are the unintended consequences of your vision to groups you may not have considered? Is your vision relevant to all learners in your community or just the dominate population? If you're not sure, seek outside opinions.

Resources to Explore

Scan the QR Code or visit https://resources.corwin.com/visioningonward to access live links to the online resources referenced in this chapter.

PART II

PRACTICAL CONSIDERATIONS AND STEPS TO VISIONING IN SCHOOLS

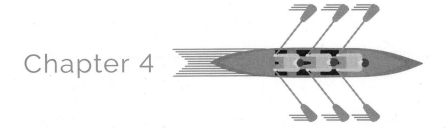

Chapter 4

VISIONING: STEPS 1–4

A vision is not just a picture of what could be; it is an appeal to our better selves, a call to become something more.

—Rosabeth Moss Kanter

Doing the Work

In Chapter 3, we shared thoughts about visioning from educational leaders and businesses.

- The University of Kansas Center for Community Health and Development portrayed visioning as your *dream—the ideal conditions.*

- Michael Fullan described the need for "irresistibly engaging technology" that is ubiquitous, efficient, and *connected to practical, everyday problem solving.*

- Cajete, a professor of Native American Studies in New Mexico, cautions that visions must be *inclusive and locally driven.*

- Research from Anthony Bryk, executive director of the Carnegie Foundation, found that "relational trust" is essential. He recommends *exploratory phases, learning from mistakes, and integrating the old with the new.*

- The vision of the Ashoka Changemaker Schools is to establish schools where *empathy is the foundation* for "solutions that are guided by humility, understanding and compassion."

In Chapter 3, we also shared the visions, adventures, and outcomes from highly successful businesses such as Amazon, Accenture, Apple, Starbucks, and Microsoft. Looking at these companies, we found their visions to be bold, in essence to "go where no one has gone before."

Building on the ideas in Chapter 3, we have designed Chapter 4 to help you obtain a bold, yet achievable, vision.

So How Will You Proceed With Visioning at Your School?

To help you end up with a vision that can be bold and yet obtainable, in this chapter we present possibilities for use with your staff. As you proceed, we urge you to also keep communication in mind, remembering at key points to reach out to those who have not been quite as involved and/or considering how to approach and engage those who disagree with the vision that is evolving. You'll find more on this subject in Chapters 5 and 6.

The *Why* of Visioning

Why are you interested in visioning?

What potential role do you think visioning has for your school?

Some Prerequisites—Biding Time, Building Trust

School leaders, visionaries, and those who are committed to improving schools may have a strong urge to rush out and create change to be on the road to strengthening schools and obtaining better outcomes. However, sometimes it is best to put on the brakes and wait patiently for the right time. Many a school leader has joined a school or been elevated to a rank within the central office staff with a deep desire to implement change. Yet, many a wise leader has taken some time to observe the comings and goings of staff, to find out about past concerns and current issues, and to build relationships and trust. Time to reflect can enhance the power of a vision.

You can imagine the devastating outcomes that might occur if a leader were to implement a timeline for visioning as if it were a goal to obtain and a benchmark to meet on a school improvement plan— particularly if this occurs without the prerequisite development of trust and deepening understanding of the staff and school community.

So, we urge you to bide your time, build trust, learn from your colleagues, and then undertake the steps that follow.

Authentic Voices

Jillayne Flanders
NAESP Distinguished Principal and Early Childhood Consultant

Early Vision and Development of a Green School

Jillayne Flanders, a former principal and leader in early childhood education in Massachusetts, describes how visioning made a difference for her school. In the 1990s, Jill found herself in the unique position of being a principal of a K–2 elementary school, a school that was run-down and obviously in need of a major overhaul. With a background in environmental science, Jill and a team of teachers from her school brought ways to learn through nature into their school within a matter of years. As they implemented their vision for children, Plains Elementary School in South Hadley, Massachusetts, was transformed into a creative world where children could count railroad ties on their hallway floor, see the impact of a rain cistern on the school roof with runnels in the ground, and view the blue pathway of a mountain stream in their lobby.

As Jill explains the process:

> My own interest in environmental science also found a home as we worked to integrate academic strands through literature. We spent almost three years on the revision and selection of our literacy programs, and then the town began to explore building a new school to replace the 80-year-old facility we were in. The architect offered the services of a school building consultant. He worked with the full faculty over the course of 4 months, and together every member of our school community had input into our vision for a child-centered early education building.

> (J. Flanders, personal communication, July 2018)

(Continued)

(Continued)

The touchstone of the building development came from one of our veteran preschool teachers, "I want this building to be a place where a four-year-old walks in and knows it was built for them." The perspective of an excited four-year-old drove almost every decision from that moment on. What was at eye level? Could everything be touched? Were the floors comfortable? How high are the toilets? Can I see myself learning? Are there places I can run, shout, and sing? Do I have a place to be quiet and cozy?

An Example of Where Visions Might Take You—Green Schools

If you are interested in environmentally friendly schools and are considering visioning to propel you forward with green innovations, visit **Online Resource 4.1** to learn more about Green Ribbon Schools. The Green Ribbon School award started in 2012. During her speech at the awards ceremony, Andrea Suarez Falken, the director of the program, stated:

> You purchase renewable energy—solar, hydro, wind, and geothermal—and generate it right on school premises. . . . Our schools include the first K–12 Platinum in the world, the first public school in the nation to achieve LEED Platinum, the first Platinum schoolhouse donated by corporate sector and the largest LEED Platinum public school in North America. You represent firsts in school certifications in Illinois, Kansas, Missouri, New York, Pennsylvania, and West Virginia. You boast one of the world's largest closed loop geothermal heating and cooling systems and the nation's first off-grid solar and wind powered school. You are Department of Energy Wind for School sites. You have achieved net zero environmental impact.
>
> You use green roofs, pervious pavement, rain gardens, rain barrels, rain cisterns, and low-flow water equipment of all types. You hold lights out lunches, implement energy management plans, and designate Helpful Energy Resource Officers (HEROs).
>
> (Falken, 2012)

Falken continues on with a list of achievements related to recycling, reduction in the use of paper and consumables, and reduction in the use of carbon fuels.

To consider progress made in the past few years, consider remarks that program director Andrea Suarez Falken made in honoring the 2018 awardees:

> You house sustainability offices; have hired sustainability directors; and implement climate action plans. You employ daylight harvesting, cool roofs, and high-efficiency heating and cooling systems, chillers, windows, and doors. You've installed rooftop solar arrays, solar water heating, cool roofs, wind turbines, geothermal, energy dashboards, high efficiency light bulbs, and digital building controls. You offer solar charging stations for personal electronic devices; budget for a green equipment purchasing account; participate in demand response programs; oversee student-supported green funds; win voter support for energy-efficient construction bonds; oversee a Solar Scholar tuition assistance fund; have gone technology-free; and purchase your power from sustainable energy sources when you do not generate it on-site. . . . You have devised landscape management, reforestation, and schoolyard master plans; and been designated Tree Schools and Tree Campuses. You've ripped up asphalt to put in green schoolyards and replaced turf with mulch and drought-resistant native plants. You feature patios, vernal pools, grottos, courtyards, ponds, multiple ecosystems, dry bed streams, and natural playgrounds of mulch, wood poles, recycled materials, stumps, tires, and climbing ropes.
>
> (Falken, 2018)

If these examples motivate you, then keep your visions for a green school in mind. Similarly, there may be other innovations that excite you. We present several at the end of this chapter. To begin, we invite you to take a step back and consider the visioning process that led to such achievements.

As you consider possible visions for your school, what do you see?

Visioning—Light-Years Beyond Ordinary (Path 1)

When it comes to visioning, there is no need to stick with the ordinary, to be constrained by budgets, to fear breaking with tradition, or to feel the need to be a follower rather than a leader along the trail. In *Leading Change*, John Kotter (1995) outlines key characteristics of an effective vision. In essence, Kotter says that in guiding the change process, leaders need to communicate a sense of urgency and involve others. According to Kotter, visions need to be succinct, have emotional appeal, and be easily communicated.

Requirements for Visions (Kotter, 1995)

- Create a sense of urgency.
- Involve others.
- Be succinct.
- Have emotional appeal.
- Be easily communicated.

When we think of the environment, and the need to reduce carbon emissions and the use of plastic, the need to assure access to water, and the potential to increase the greening of America, the possibilities of introducing scientifically validated procedures in schools are endless. When we consider technology and 21st century learning, innovations for STEAM and creative expansion of how technology is integrated into learning, the possibilities for schools are numerous and evolving. When we consider the extent of violence, the loss of social communication skills with the advent of a hyperfocus on digital media, and the degree of escapism that is occurring with opioid and other drug addiction, the need for schools to focus on more than high-pressure options to increase academic skills is readily apparent. Before we dive into our recommended sequence for visioning, we would like to provide more ideas from school leaders. Next we provide a second glimpse into the vision and visioning process at the Rainbow Community School (see also the introduction).

Authentic Voice

Visioning at the Rainbow Community School in Asheville, North Carolina

In the introduction to this book, we highlighted the vision of Rainbow Community School, a vision for co-creation and harmony, created by circles of visioning with participation from school leaders and staff, families, and the broader Asheville community. To arrive at its current and ever-evolving vision, the Rainbow community is involved in *dynamic governance* sociocracy. Using a web model, Rainbow School is always visioning through general circles with educators, students, parents, and families. You can read more about this process at the Creative Learning Solutions website where you will find an article, "Dynamic Governance"; see <u>Online Resource 4.2.</u>

Its mission is to "develop accomplished, confident, and creative learners who are prepared to be compassionate leaders in building a socially just, spiritually connected, and environmentally sustainable world." As Dr. Renee Owen, the executive director since 2007, explains, "We inspire academic excellence with a program in harmony with the stages of child development. We model within our community the kind of world in which we aspire to live." The Rainbow Community School's (n.d.) website provides additional information on its *holistic* approach:

> Holistic Education follows this same premise [that life is an interaction of wholes rather than a collection of individual parts], subscribing to the philosophy that the learning experience is a comprehensive integration not only of traditional academic subjects, but of the many facets that comprise a human being. The reductionist view that humans are simply a mind/body construct—a machine with parts that can be modified in isolation—does not fulfill the learner's true potential.

> Indeed, humans are far more intricate, subtle and mysterious beings. We are multi-faceted creatures with a range of complex emotions, deep connections to the natural world, seekers of the mystery, with an innate need to create, to share, to understand & to be understood. It is the Holistic view that recognizes this concept and the Holistic Education model that seeks its implementation—for the enrichment of the "whole" learner.

> Yet, before we can truly nurture the "whole" learner, we must define those individual facets, much in the way that a prism defines white light into seven bands of color. At Rainbow Community School (RCS), the student is viewed Holistically through Seven Domains: spiritual, mental, social, emotional, creative, natural, and physical. The purpose of this education model is to develop the whole learner

(Continued)

(Continued)

into a healthy, intelligent, compassionate, creative, and productive human who is capable of leading an empowered and enriched life.

The vision at Rainbow Community School evolved over the past forty years. According to Dr. Owen, "It is all transactional. . . . Educators need trust and a space to be creative that the bureaucracy is not allowing for" (R. Owen, personal communication, 2017). Dr. Owen indicated that at Rainbow Community School, they viewed visioning as a process of co-creating and finding meaning and purpose.

As the Center for Educational Improvement indicated in one of its 2018 blogs,

Students are thirsting for something more. How many times do students ask if they will use something in real life? By linking individuals to their own mountaintop experiences, their sense of awe or connection to a greater purpose, students have the opportunity to learn more about themselves and to experience the deep satisfaction that comes from connecting to their own inner wisdom.

(Barrows & Mason, 2018)

As explained at the Atlas Society website,

Our self-reflective, creative capacity is the nature and source of the human *spirit*—of those things that arise from our unique form of consciousness. We are the creators, the motive force, the prime movers of our own moral characters, of our own knowledge, of our own world. . . . Properly understood, then, the spiritual is that which pertains to our human capacities for understanding, self-awareness, free will, and moral responsibility.

(Hudgins, 2011)

Another Need—Visioning to Handle a Crisis (Path 2)

As we take you through the steps to visioning, it may be helpful to consider a two-fold path to visioning. For the most part, we will be discussing *Path 1: Visioning to Innovate*; however, as Paul Liabenow reminds us, visioning is sometimes needed to handle emergencies or crises (*Path 2: Visioning in Times of Crisis*). As a superintendent, Paul was in a situation where there seemed to be an epidemic of suicides. Whether it is suicides, school shootings, bullying, a spike in drug abuse, gang involvement, or other deeply troubling situations, sometimes visioning needs to occur to move beyond Band-Aids. In Paul's case, he followed the steps in this chapter but moved at an accelerated pace.

Our takeaway from Paul's experience is that visioning isn't only about dreams for an exciting innovation, sometimes it is desperately needed to help a school community move beyond tragedies to turn the tide in the face of unspeakable sorrow or to help reestablish a sense of hope for the future.

Key Learning 4.1

Why Is Your School Beginning the Visioning Process?

☐ To innovate

☐ To respond to a crisis

☐ To improve school culture

☐ To become trauma-informed

☐ To meet the changing needs of staff and students

☐ To improve academic achievement

☐ To create a school ideal for my community

Path 2: Visioning in Times of Crisis

Dr. Paul Liabenow
CEI President and Executive Director of MEMSPA

Experiences in Michigan

As a superintendent in Cadillac, Michigan, Paul Liabenow faced a rash of teenage suicides. Over a period of five short years, six teens had elected to end their own lives. To address this situation, Paul moved into high gear to work with trusted leaders to not only find a solution to end the suicides but also to help address underlying needs and issues. With a team of principals, teachers, counselors, and

(Continued)

(Continued)

key community leaders, a visioning team identified what a safe and secure school system would look like. Paul and the Cadillac School District began to gather professionals on the topic of teen suicide—including psychiatrists, psychologists, and bullying prevention experts—to identify adolescent risk factors that may have led to the multiple tragedies. A community focus group was developed to review school districts and community needs and resources. After several months of collaborative work, new resources and supports were added to the school and community. They started initiatives including a Challenge Day, which provided suicide prevention training for students, teachers, and parents; aggression prevention training for students, teachers, and community members; and opportunities for student mentoring and relationship building. The end result was a more positive culture and climate in the school district and community.

Key Learning 4.2

Are There Any Crises in Your School That You Need to Respond To?

☐ Student and/or staff suicide(s)

☐ Drug and/or alcohol abuse

☐ Extreme poverty

☐ Neighborhood violence

☐ Racial, social, or economic inequity

☐ Discrimination

☐ Low academic achievement

☐ Low teacher morale and/or high attrition

☐ High number of suspensions and expulsions

☐ Lack of parent involvement

☐ Parental incarceration

Considerations for the Visioning Process

Path 1: Visioning—A Circle of Ideas

You may have noticed that so far, we have not given you a formula for visioning. We have not narrowed visioning down to a tightly woven process. However, we have provided some far-ranging ideas. We have organized the visions we presented in Chapter 2 in a circle of ideas (see Figure 4.1).

Figure 4.1   Circle of Ideas

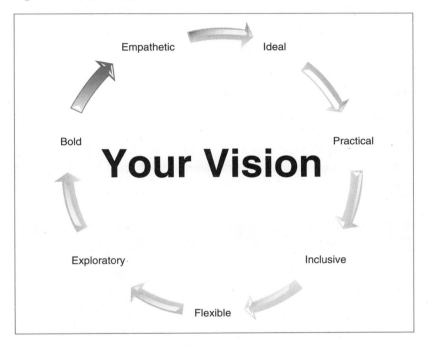

Looking at the circle of ideas that summarizes major themes for the research we have undertaken on visioning, we find much in common with recommendations from the Pickett Institute. Created by the Institute of Law and Justice in Virginia in partnership with the Bureau of Justice Assistance and the Office of Justice Programs' Statewide Community Initiative, the Pickett Institute Curriculum was designed for community-based planning and capacity building.

Building on Kotter's concepts of visioning, The Pickett Institute (2002) describes the characteristics of visioning this way:

- **Imaginable**: Conveying a picture of the future

- **Desirable**: Appealing to and inspiring employees, customers, and others who are stakeholders

- **Feasible**: Including realistic, attainable goals

- **Focused**: Clear enough to provide guidance in decision-making

- **Flexible**: General enough to allow individual initiative and alternative responses in light of changing conditions

- **Communicable**: Easy to understand and communicate; can be successfully explained in two minutes (p. 2)

An Initial Checklist

To help you get started with visioning, spend a few minutes considering your vision using the *Initial Checklist for Creating a Vision for Your School* that we present in Key Learning 4.3. Note that this exercise is designed to help leaders clarify your own views prior to visioning with others at your school.

Key Learning 4.3

Initial Checklist for Creating a Vision for Your School

Imagine the future. Write three or four key sentences about your vision for the future for your school.

Are you looking at Path 1 (Innovation) or Path 2 (A Crisis)?
Do you have a deadline you are trying to meet? If so, what is it?
What difference will your vision make?

Check your vision:

☐ 1. Is it inspirational to teachers and other staff?

☐ 2. Is it inspirational to key stakeholders (parents, students, board of education)?

☐ 3. Is it bold?

☐ 4. Is it empathetic?

☐ 5. Is it inclusive?

☐ 6. Is it feasible? Are goals attainable?

☐ 7. Is it focused?

☐ 8. Does it provide guidance for decision-making?

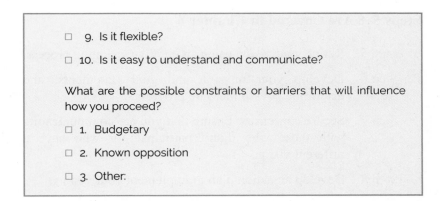

☐ 9. Is it flexible?

☐ 10. Is it easy to understand and communicate?

What are the possible constraints or barriers that will influence how you proceed?

☐ 1. Budgetary

☐ 2. Known opposition

☐ 3. Other:

So, What Will You Do to Vision at Your School?

Now that you have some background on visioning and have written down some of your own thoughts on your vision (see Initial Checklist), let's get practical. We have organized this chapter so that we begin with an overview of the steps. After that, we provide some additional recommendations that will help you address the *how* of visioning.

A Recommended Eight-Step Visioning Process

Note to readers: Do not begin the steps in this chapter until you have previewed Chapters 4–6. You will want to understand the entire process prior to beginning visioning as a team in your school/district.

Steps 1–4 Will Be Reviewed in This Chapter

Step 1: Form a vision steering team, and develop a blueprint for your visioning process.

Step 2: Determine who will be involved in visioning—consider community stakeholders, teachers, school staff, and maybe even students. Consider how to allow all voices to be heard *by each other*, not just the decision makers or administrators.

Step 3: Develop your first draft of your vision. Imagine your school the way you would like it to be.

Step 4: Research exemplars and options.

Steps 5–8 Are Covered in Chapter 6

Step 5:   Refine your vision using an iterative visioning process.

Step 6:   Develop your mission and goal statements, and determine how to measure progress.

Step 7:   Secure consensus. Ensure that you are communicating with those who didn't participate or who have a different vision.

Step 8:   Develop an action plan to implement your vision.

Our recommended visioning process is iterative in that it has a path for cycling back, revisiting draft visions, and revising your early vision (see Figure 4.2). The iterative visioning process can be completed by

Figure 4.2   Visioning Process: Steps 1–8

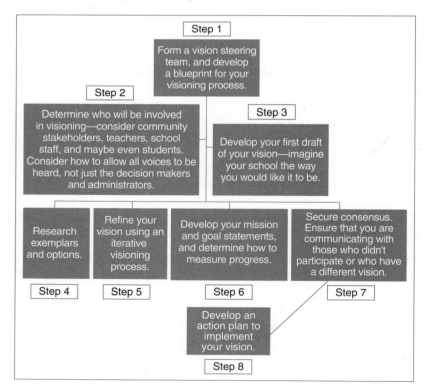

an individual or by a small or large group. Often one person or a small group of people may start the visioning process by following the steps in this chapter. This is, in part, a test run. Just as you might test drive a car before purchasing one, visioning by one person or a small group provides a way to try out the process prior to deciding how to involve the larger group in visioning. (See Chapter 6 for steps to refine your vision.) Visioning involves a process of multiplexing ideas about the future so that innovations are explored, communicated, and implemented with an authentic sense that we have held fast to some underlying principles and truths to expand possibilities for our students.

Step 1—Form a Vision Steering Team, and Develop a Visioning Process Blueprint

So, who do you want on your steering team? We recommend that you consider two or three individuals. You might look to a couple of your department heads, your assistant principal, and perhaps a parent or community leader. You want to include people who can help you capture the pulse of your school community—its needs, frustrations, dreams, and potential. Look for people who are creative, progressive, and perhaps even those who know their field well. You want people you can trust, who will share openly with you, and who will also be influence wielders with their peers. The people you select should understand the importance of this activity and be able to devote sufficient time to it over the course of one to two years. Ideally you will have a group in which you can toss around a few ideas as you explore the potential of this visioning work. You may even want to consider appointing one of your team members as the lead to head up the steering team. Make sure you have someone designated to keep notes from your meeting and to help keep the steering team organized. Also consider a place, such as Google Docs, to electronically store notes, minutes from meetings, and ideas.

You will want the initial group to be supporters of the visioning process (see Figure 4.3). If any person you have selected is hesitant, you may want to consider replacing that individual with someone who is more likely to help encourage and promote the visioning you are about to undertake.

Considering the type and magnitude of change that a vision requires will lead you to who needs to be at the table. As you consider the players, map out what value they bring to the team. What credibility level will they hold with your stakeholders? How open are they to idea sharing? Will they be a driver for the shared vision that's created, even if it isn't their own original thinking?

Figure 4.3   Potential Steering Team Members

Name	Title	Team Role	Credibility With Stakeholders	Openness

Key Learning 4.4

Understanding Where to Begin With a Needs Assessment

Before you can decide what to do to make the changes you want in your school or district, you have to understand what students, teachers, staff/faculty, and parents feel that they need. The more robust your needs assessment, the more valuable that information will be in guiding your action plan. You can do a simple survey asking the school community to rate their satisfaction with aspects of how you run your school or district. Many districts have a regular practice of distributing such surveys to families on a yearly basis. Using these results can help you make choices that will satisfy your educational community.

To do a more robust needs assessment, your steering team will need to look at a variety of data and analyze your school's or district's strengths and weaknesses. Considering academic achievement, attendance records, suspension and detention rates, and school climate can give you a more holistic picture of exactly how your school or district can improve. Using the *School Compassionate Culture Analytic Tool for Educators (S-CCATE)* is one option that will identify your school's strengths, weaknesses, and comparison to a nationally normed group as well as providing you with ideas for improvement through professional development and intervention suggestions. Completing this process will ensure that your school is changing in ways that make sense for its needs.

It is becoming more common for teachers to analyze student data, so this wouldn't necessarily be an "extra" task that teachers must do but rather being more mindful about how data can be used to create their vision and stepping back from the data to think about the school or district as a whole.

Before the Visioning Process Begins

Prior to the first meeting, circulate a brief email with references (and links) to a few creative ideas. You could build on ideas in this book. Ask a provocative question and secure team members' agreement to attend the first session.

To begin the process, explain your rationale, draft a blueprint and timeline, and ask those present to take a few minutes to record their ideas for a vision for your school. You may even want the group to reflect on this over the course of a week and then meet again to share ideas. At the beginning of this chapter, we presented several ideas that may serve as a catalyst or provide an engaging activity for initial visioning. Your group may also want to consider the "Resources and Ideas to Support the *How* of Visioning" at the end of this chapter for guidance on how they will vision together with others at your school.

At that first meeting, your team will consider not only the blueprint for visioning but also a strategy for communications, including how and how much to share with others. The way you proceed will vary according to factors such as perceived barriers, degrees of resistance to change among your staff, the amount of pressure, and staff morale at your school.

To work with the steering team, you may want to practice some of the activities that you will take to others, beginning with the Community Tool Box exercise.

Key Learning 4.5

Community Tool Box

For this first step, imagine your school the way you would like it to be. Write out your ideas. Don't worry about how they sound. This is sort of like a personal brainstorming session—get everything in your head out on paper without judging it. You can clarify and focus later. Use the questions adapted from the Community Tool Box (a resource provided by the Center for Community Health and Development at the University of Kansas, to help guide your process (Axner, 2018)—see **Online Resource 4.3** Developing and Communicating a Vision by Marya Axner.

What does your school community look like physically? What kind of buildings are there? What kind of public spaces? Is it safe to walk around it during the day?

(Continued)

(Continued)

What do teachers and other staff do at your school?

Do teachers and staff like their work? Why or why not?

Do students like the school, its offerings, and its teachers/staff? Why or why not?

How do people get along with each other? Do people from different groups communicate and get along? Do younger and older people have contact and good relationships with each other?

How do decisions get made? Are things fair for different groups? Does every group have a fair say? Are many people involved in sharing their ideas and solving problems?

What do families look like? Do people within families get along? Are there places where women and men can get help if they need it? Is there child care available? Do single people, extended families, traditional families, and nontraditional families feel there is a place for them in the school community? Are people from various cultures and ethnic groups at your school? If so, do they get along? Is your school warm and welcoming to all?

Who does your school serve? How many students? What ages? Do students come from one or multiple neighborhoods? How far do students travel to school?

Do people in the community go to recreational events at your school? What possibilities are there for young people, old people, and everybody in between?

Capture answers to these questions, and store them electronically under the title Community Tool Box, Initial Questions.

In addition to the questions in the Community Tool Box, we suggest that you also consider these issues at this stage:

What are the primary concerns that are a catalyst to possible innovation or reform (e.g., student achievement; discipline, bullying, violence, a crisis, or an emergency in your community; outdated materials or methods; interest in a particular innovation such as STEM; or a need to update technology)?

What possible support or opposition to change do you have in your school or district?

What community, national, or international trends and concerns might affect your school or district?

What are the potential outcomes that might be achieved if the vision were implemented?

What are the possible costs and benefits or cost-effectiveness of implementing the vision? In estimating this, focus on cost and benefits the first year, the second year, and five years out.

From this activity, proceed to develop a goal statement and a timeline, perhaps with a two- or three-day retreat or with monthly meetings over a period of several months. If you are introducing ideas that may be considered radical and a serious departure from previous operations, or if there are factors that are contributing to low staff morale or community concerns about your school or district, you will want to ensure that there is adequate time for reflection and revisiting ideas.

Key Learning 4.6

Steering Team Commitment Creation

Goal of the Steering Team:

Steering Team's First Meeting:

Steering Team will meet _____ times a week or month.

First Meeting Agenda:

What's going well in the school community?

What are the sacred rituals, traditions, or beliefs that should not be shifted because they have systemic value or because they are a core thread in the multiplexing matrix that supports the foundational structure of many other components?

What beliefs, practices, and core values are already in place that will elevate the ultimate vision? Allowing stakeholders to affirm past practices is refreshing and energizing. It's a subtle way to say, "because of this, now we can . . ."

Often change is viewed as innovative, or a leap of faith, when it is actually the courage to move ahead based on where you have been and the knowledge that came before your current thinking. Thanks to our experiences, good and bad, we can move forward with clarity and confidence that we are doing what's right for our students.

Over the course of visioning, the steering team will meet periodically to review progress and reflect on implications and recommendations for next steps. Many ideas will flow, some will resonate with this core group, and others won't be a match. The importance of these discussions is that every idea is considered; all are heard. A vision created in isolation of collective voice will be shallow and unheard. Prioritizing the steering team meetings will keep everyone at the table in a collective mode of growth-minded movement. It's easy to get busy and allow this critical leadership layer to dissolve. Make sure you are talking, exploring, thinking, and taking action on behalf of shared perspectives.

Blueprint

Your blueprint will include a timeline and suggested activities. This might include events such as the following:

- An invitational meeting to explore ideas, be provocative, and secure commitment

- Ideas for activities that might occur at each session (see the exercises at the end of Chapter 3)

- Initial thoughts about concerns that are likely to arise, their possible validity, and how you might problem solve and address concerns

- Possible ways to evaluate the impact of your activity (participant satisfaction, any implementation)

Step 2—Identify Participants for the Visioning Process

Once you have worked with your steering team and established an initial blueprint for your visioning, the next step is to identify who will participate in your school's or district's visioning process.

Individual schools have conducted visioning with the total faculty and key auxiliary staff, or they have worked with a smaller group of individuals. We believe there is value in working with all teaching and key auxiliary staff (such as deans of students, school psychologists, and counselors). You may want to involve district staff such as technology or curriculum coordinators. You also may want to include parent and community representatives.

Step 3—Develop the First Draft of Your Vision, and Imagine Your School the Way You Would Like It to Be

When you hold your first visioning meeting, consider some of the options listed in the "Resources and Ideas to Support the *How* of Visioning" in this chapter for creative ways to engage participants. Divide into teams so that each group includes a maximum of eight or nine people. We find it helpful if the teams meet and then share back with others ideas about their involvement. You may wish to use an outside consultant with experience in leading visioning sessions to facilitate visioning. Ensure that you have someone tasked with keeping notes and furthering communication with the participants. Start by considering the ideal, without concerns regarding budget or possible opposition. Visions are stronger when they begin from a place without constraints.

Once ideas have been shared and discussed, a process of voting or polling can be used to help narrow down possibilities. Identifying thirty examples of vision statements, TopNonprofits (2017) suggests that "the best visions are inspirational, clear, memorable, and concise."

In Chapter 1, we provided examples of vision statements from several schools and districts. Here are a few additional statements:

Frost Elementary School (Cumberland, MD): "The vision at Frost Elementary School is to prepare and motivate our students for a rapidly changing world by instilling in them critical thinking skills, a global perspective, and a respect for core values of honesty, loyalty, perseverance, and compassion. Students will have success for today and be prepared for tomorrow" (Allegany Public Schools, 2019).

Hart High School (Santa Clarita, CA): "Hart High is dedicated to a continuing tradition of excellence in an ever-changing world. Within a safe and supportive environment, we provide a relevant, high-quality education, and prepare our diverse student body for future endeavors. We honor achievement and promote pride in ourselves, in our school, and in our community" (Hart High School, n.d.).

Spring City Elementary School (Spring City, PA): Our school vision: "Be safe. Be respectful. Be responsible. Be awesome!" (S. Choi and M. Patschke, personal communication, 2018).

Upper Providence Elementary School (Royersford, PA): "UPE is an engaging environment where everyone is acknowledged, valued, and matters. We support the whole child and the 'team sport' of teaching & learning. We care. We laugh. We collectively believe in the life-changing power of our school community" (M. Patschke, personal communication, 2012).

Step 4—Research Exemplars and Options

The fourth step involves the identification and review of exemplars, which are schools that demonstrate successful implementation of visions similar to the one you are considering. This step is important for your vision because it can provide inspiration and some structural guidance. Allow the exemplars to guide you into forming a vision that is unique to your own school's needs and aspirations. This process can be completed by beginning with quick review, followed by more extensive follow-up.

- For the quick approach, educators at your school will identify exemplars through research and discussion with others.

- We suggest that a designated team research options over a period of time, with periodic reports back to others.

- For the extended approach, educators will follow up with visits or discussions with exemplary schools after their initial research.

For this process, a small group from your visioning team may wish to take on the responsibility of conducting this background research and reporting back to others. This is likely to take several months.

> ## Key Learning 4.7
>
> *How to Review Exemplars*
>
> 1. **What is the visioning statement for the school or district?**
>
> 2. **How is it being implemented?**
>
> 3. **Find out the history:**
>
>   What was the catalyst for visioning?
>
>   Was it a crisis or a desire for innovation?
>
>   Were others influential in moving forward with visioning? If so, who and what was their concern?
>
>   Who was involved in the visioning process?
>
>   How were barriers addressed?
>
> 4. **What advice do they have for others?**
>
> 5. **How did they pay for visioning activities? For implementation?**
>
> 6. **At this point in time, how cost-effective is visioning? Do they have suggestions for reducing costs?**
>
> 7. **If they were to do it again, what might they do differently?**
>
> 8. **Were some aspects of visioning more effective than others?**
>
> 9. **What advice do they have for others?**

To help you begin the exemplar review, the following paragraphs briefly describe some key ideas from recent trends that have specific relevance to schools of the future. *Think of your school as you read though these examples; try to vision what it may become if you were able to incorporate some of these new tactics into its curriculum. Once you are finished, complete Key Learning 4.8.*

Examples—The Future of Schools

One exemplar for schools of the future comes from recommendations from Sheryl Nussbaum-Beach (2011), a board member of ISTE and 21st century learning consultant, in an article for the

Association for Supervision and Curriculum Development (ASCD) titled, "A Futuristic Vision for 21st Century Education." This article alerts educators about the rapid growth of technology and how the students of today learn not only from teachers and books but technology as well. The internet provides us with endless amounts of information, which is why 21st century education must shift from being content-based to being based on guidance in how to effectively process and critically examine the sea of information that is always at our fingertips.

Nussbaum-Beach developed a three-pronged approach to 21st century learning:

1. **Learning face-to-face.** We must build trusting relationships with others so that we can feel comfortable sharing new and unconventional ideas. This is especially important in the face of technology growth because many of our relationships and connections are formed through the internet, depriving us from important face-to-face interactions.
2. **Learning through global communities of inquiry.** The importance of face-to-face interactions does not mean that communities formed in virtual space are harmful. Connecting with people across the globe who share the same vision can only help it grow. This type of learning helps us become comfortable with cultural differences because it soon becomes clear that we are not so different after all.
3. **Building a personal learning network (PLN).** A PLN is the way in which we learn through the vast resources provided to us by new technology.

These steps can help guide teachers down the path of the 21st century. We must envision what we want our schools to become because "we are not marching slowly into the future, we are speeding toward it in a whirlwind frenzy, mandated by the exponential rate of change" (Nussbaum-Beach, 2011).

Considering 21st Century Instruction. Nussbaum-Beach suggests three criteria for what should be included in instructions to students:

- "Fluid, shaping, and reshaping itself in response to students' self-direction and unpredictable events"

- Designed to provide students opportunities to "build relationships, network, and act collectively"

- Inclusive of activities that require that students synthesize information and demonstrate self-reliance

Personalizing 21st Century Education. Daniel A. Domenech, executive director of the American Association of School Administrators, recently coauthored a book, *Personalizing 21st Century Education: A Framework for Student Success*, with Morton Sherman and John L. Brown (2016). In that book, Domenech et al. ask a few key questions:

- What if we were asked to imagine a world in which the educational system revolved around teaching a single student?

- In this world for a single student, how much of the current system would remain? Would we need classrooms and school buildings? Would all students be expected to graduate in thirteen years? Would we need to assess all students at the same time with the same tests? Would we need report cards and grades? Would we be able to close the achievement gap? Would we need remedial services, summer school, after-school programs, and the practice of not promoting students to the next grade?

- How would the role of the teacher change?

Reconceptualizing the Role of Technology in Schools. In a 2012 article in *Principal*, Nancy Blair, a former school improvement consultant and current principal at Rising Starr Middle School in Fayetteville, Georgia, suggests that new technologies are setting the stage for a vital shift in teacher and student roles in which teachers become catalysts to learning, spending less time creating presentations and more time crafting powerful learning activities. With this approach, Blair envisions that material will be covered in more depth with better retention as students use technology and drive instruction by being explorers and designers.

Although many educational innovations involve technology, there are other innovations that may be impactful, such as music, art, book fairs, science exhibits, and other ways to move beyond a strictly academically based innovation.

Music and Sound in Schools

Close your eyes, and picture your school. Then add a layer of sound to your visualization. What do you hear? Is it music? Noise? Silence?

Music can be an effective way to affect mood, and choosing background music to accompany transitional periods can have a powerful influence on the atmosphere of a group. Music is also a powerful tool to incorporate into classes when varying degrees of distraction are used to imprint and test learned information (Dolegui, 2013). Some children learn better with earplugs and some with headphones with music playing softly in the background as they study. Research even shows that making music together, especially through singing, can have beneficial effects on blood pressure and anxiety and can even improve well-being and health (Stollznow, 2011).

Mitigating sound in traditionally noisy and echo-filled areas, such as large hallways, cafeterias, and gymnasiums, is also an important consideration when controlling volume levels in learning environments. Adjusting the sound levels of classroom spaces is something that can contribute greatly to better learning. Creating a quiet space for students to use within each classroom is a simple and effective way to encourage a personally directed sense of self-care and self-control.

(A. Dilger, personal communication, April 15, 2017)

Using Engineering and Design Thinking to Develop a New Vision

Shelly Goldman and Molly Zielezinski (2016), in *Developing New Vision and Approaches to Twenty-First Century Learning*, describe how technology will drive a shift in the role of teachers. With greater use of technology, Blair believes teachers will be freed to shift to a more holistic approach to education. Instead of focusing as much on the subject matter, teachers will become empathetic, will employ more engineering and design thinking, and will help students do the following:

- Learn that failure is a positive aspect of the learning process. (This is part of the Plan, Do, Check, Act Cycle of engineering education—see Figure 4.4.)

- Experience the positives of collaboration.

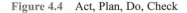

Figure 4.4   Act, Plan, Do, Check

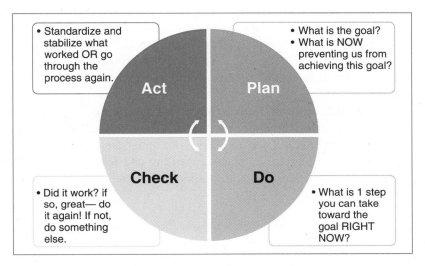

At the beginning of this chapter we provided several examples from Green Ribbon Schools. Other examples of STEAM initiatives include exemplars for technology, engineering, and math. Explore these valuable resources on our online resource page.

- **Online Resource 4.4** US Department of Education Science, Technology, Engineering, and Math Initiative

- **Online Resource 4.5** Battelle for Kids 21st Century Learning Exemplar Program

- **Online Resource 4.6** Next Generation Science Standards

- **Online Resource 4.7** National Council of Teachers of Mathematics—Publications

- **Online Resource 4.8** National Council of Teachers of Mathematics—Grants

- **Online Resource 4.9** The Engineers' Council—Tech Trek

A Unifying Aim for Developing Better Adults. Nel Noddings (2015), an educational philosopher and professor emerita at Stanford University, suggests that the future will see a shift away from quantifiable measures of performance, which have been used as a means of achieving financial security. Instead, Noddings suggests that the new vision of schools will encompass all aspects of student's lives: intellectual, physical, moral, spiritual, social, vocational, aesthetic, and civic. From that new vision, Noddings believes increased collegiality among students and teachers, more cross-disciplinary themes, and enriched curricula that addresses homemaking and parenting will emerge.

The Application of Neuroscience in Classrooms. The field of neuroscience, with the application of the science of how children learn, offers an exciting way to deepen our understanding of learning and to apply strategies that enhance learning and academic achievement. Here are some of the most important findings from recent research:

- Learning is influenced by executive functions within the brain (Zelazo, Carlson, & Kesek, 2008).

- Today, we can measure working memory, attention, distractibility, cognitive flexibility, response lag, and other executive functions through the NIH Toolbox, which includes scales that can be administered on iPads and tablets (Zelazo et al., 2008).

- Children who are most behind on measures of executive functioning (i.e., children who are the most disadvantaged, have disabilities, or have experienced significant trauma) benefit the most from executive functioning interventions and programs (Flook et al., 2010).

- Stress and trauma negatively affect executive functioning, and mindfulness and meditation can improve brain functioning by creating plasticity in the regions of the brain that fosters emotional regulation (Hölzel et al., 2011).

- Emotional regulation is a critical life skill that is developmental. Stress, poverty, and trauma all can negatively affect emotional regulation (Martin & Ochsner, 2016).

In addition to these visions for the future, there are at least a dozen more ways that the future of schools may be shaped by current research and trends—trends not only in education but in science, technology, and other fields. These can be discovered online or through networking with others. Resources such as newsletters or websites provided by educational associations or other educational organizations sometimes include exemplars in their articles. Find exemplars that resonate with your school and its vision. Subscribe to the Center for Educational Improvement's (CEI's) *Wow! Ed Newsletter* to get the latest evidenced-based interventions, responses to educational concerns, and examples of what's working in schools around the world.

Key Learning 4.8

Researching Exemplar Schools—Exemplar Educational Approaches

We recommend that this be completed as exemplars are reviewed with staff at your school.

Innovative Approach/School	Description/Link for More Info	What Is Unique and Appealing?

Researching Options—The Extended Exercise

Once you have completed the "quick" part of Step 2, reviewing exemplars, you may find it valuable to dig a little deeper by selecting certain schools or approaches that you will review in more detail. Here are a few steps that you may find to be helpful:

1. Use a procedure to verify which exemplars are most appealing to your faculty/staff. You could use a simple voting or consensus procedure or a procedure such as nominal voting, whereby participants are given a specified number of dots to vote for their favorite options, which are posted on a board or wall. Participants sometimes are given options to either spread their dots among the alternatives or to load up on a few as they complete their voting.
2. Follow up with visits to schools using the most popular approaches.
3. Attend meetings and webinars where these ideas will be presented.
4. In discussions with key leaders for these activities, make sure to get two to three contacts to connect with so that you can assess the feedback from people who have used or are actively applying the particular approach.
5. At some point you will want to review the ideas in "Resources and Ideas to Support the *How* of Visioning" as well as ideas presented in the first twenty pages of this chapter to consider which group activities to include in your visioning process.

Conclusions—Borrowing From the Greats

Good teachers know that borrowing ideas, materials, and resources that work from other educators and making them their own can reduce their workload, inspire them and their students, and build on collective knowledge. Instead of starting from scratch, reflect on whether your school is visioning because of a school or community crisis or because you're ready to innovate. Once you know which path you're on, research schools that had similar needs and successfully transformed their culture to meet those needs. We've provided some examples of exemplar schools in this and subsequent chapters, but getting on the ground and talking to school leaders at schools in your city, state, or country is an invaluable exercise.

Practical Points to Ponder

- Visioning can occur in response to a question for innovation (Path 1) or crisis (Path 2).

- Early on, line up support with a visioning steering team.

- Review the current status and the history of the school to consider factors that may support or detract from visioning.

- To obtain buy-in make sure that many are involved in the visioning process.

- With iterative visioning, the vision may shift as participants take additional steps to delve more deeply into visioning.

- Take the time to research exemplars.

- Consider an array of factors, including costs, but do not let costs drive your vision.

No matter which path you take to develop and pursue a vision, it is important to be inclusive—inclusive in identifying your steering team and inclusive as you go about the visioning process. Your vision, however, will be stronger, when you are inclusive and when your school or district operates from a frame of knowledge, research, and deep understanding. This will take time.

Ideas for Leading and Learning

- There are a variety of ways to kick off visioning and to help participants consider options (see the first twenty pages of this chapter as well as "Resources and Ideas to Support the *How* of Visioning." *What is most appealing and why?*

- Visioning sometimes begins with pilots with certain grade levels or subjects. *Is your vision a better fit for certain grade levels or subjects? If so, why?*

- A review of exemplars can be completed in six to twelve weeks and may or may not include visits to the exemplary sites. *What are the possible implications not only for the best-fit grade levels and subjects, but for others?*

(Continued)

(Continued)

- Communities can be involved at steps along the way. *How will you involve parents and community members? How much support are you likely to garner from them? What of opposition? How will this be handled?*

- Time, money, and attitudes are usually barriers to success. *What are the barriers, how significant are these barriers, and are there potential strategies to reduce resistance?*

- Over time, as visions are implemented, they change with results and obstacles that appear. *What shifts are likely to occur as you pursue and implement the vision?*

- When pursuing a vision, an important factor is its sustainability. *What about the likely sustainability? What factors are indicative of sustainability of your proposed vision?* (Consider degree of buy-in/ opposition, other factors competing for time and attention, and the stability of leadership at your school/district).

Although we will cover this in greater detail in Chapter 7, leaders who begin with a conscious awareness of sustainability—including both barriers and also factors that will lead to greater sustainability— may find fewer frustrations as the inevitable barriers arise during the visioning process. These will be further explored in the next chapter.

Resources and Ideas to Support the *How* of Visioning

Although we will delve further into models for visioning throughout this book, here are a few alternative ways to conduct visioning. Several of these ideas come from the Pickett Institute's (2002) article on "The Power of Visioning in Strategic Planning."

Visioning Retreats

Consider a vision retreat with key stakeholders (teachers, staff, parents, students). Some schools or districts start with a retreat with a small cross-section of stakeholders—perhaps key teacher leaders and representatives from other groups. Retreats are valuable because they provide a way to step away from the daily grind for participants to enter a space free from the pressures of normal daily life to consider steps beyond the ordinary day to day. During your retreat, you may be able to conduct some of the following exercises to help begin and guide your visioning.

Cover Story Visioning

Imagine being featured in a major magazine in the future. How will your organization or project be described?

Allow this to be a brainstorm; don't hold anything back! In the beginning stages, it is important to get all the ideas out. Then, later on in the process, you can choose the best and most practical ones. As long as your vision feels powerful and appears clear in your mind, it is something worth sharing (The Pickett Institute, 2002).

Hot Air Balloon Visioning

Imagine that you have come back to your neighborhood after ten years have passed. You are floating over it. What do you see?

Both this exercise and cover story visioning require strong imaginations. Here it is important to get in touch with yourself and imagine what you truly want your school to be. Overthinking can impede this process. These exercises invite participants to be creative and suspend judgment while they imagine the potential for what could be under ideal circumstances.

Exploring Metaphors and Stories

Explore metaphors and stories that describe the future organization. What was it that inspired you to go into the school system? Was it someone's story about how a school changed his or her life? Did a powerful experience of your own play a role in shaping your ambitions? Questions such as these can help you realize why your vision is important to you and what it needs to be.

Creating Visioning Maps

Create a vision map that integrates information about vision elements, values, critical issues, and competencies. This can be similar

Figure 4.6   Example of Part of a Visioning Map

to a Venn diagram; start with your school in the center of the page, allow the elements of your vision to branch off from there, and watch it grow right before your eyes. The vision map in Figure 4.6 is for Langley School District in Langley, a suburb of Vancouver, British Columbia. To learn more about the Langley visioning process, visit their website at **Online Resource 4.10.**

Iterative Visioning

Whether you use visioning maps, metaphors, cover stories, or other approaches to stimulating visions, we believe that iterative, or repeated visioning, is important, and that the best visions are developed over time, with opportunities for dialogue, reflection, and re-visioning.

CEI has developed an iterative approach to 21st century learning that seeks to help schools become more compassionate. This is one approach to visioning. We will show you how the approach can be adapted to fit specific needs and interests of schools.

As CEI guides schools in visioning, we begin with an iterative visioning process through use of S-CCATE (Mason, Rivers Murphy,

Bergey, et al., 2018). S-CCATE is a forty-item diagnostic instrument that teams of teachers and school leaders can use to vision, plan, evaluate their school, make decisions for school improvement, and continually refine their approach. The S-CCATE has five scales—leadership and a compassionate school community, conscious awareness of emotions and stress, courage and resiliency, confidence and positivity, and understanding of equity—and includes an online version for data aggregation.

Heart Centered Learning® (see Figure 4.7) is one approach to visioning. As advanced by CEI, Heart Centered Learning begins with a visioning process completed by small groups of teacher leaders in a school using core learning teams as advocated by Peter Senge (Senge, 2006; Senge et al., 2012). To recreate schools as Heart Centered Communities requires an intensive effort to refocus schools and school cultures where students become immersed in environments that consider socio-emotional well-being and the needs of self and

Figure 4.7   Heart Centered Learning

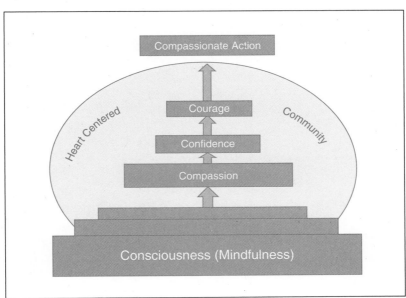

others. In this way, positive relationships are deepened, cooperation is expanded, and students gain confidence and courage to act in ways that enhance their own lives as well as the lives of others.

Resources to Explore

Scan the QR Code or visit https://resources.corwin.com/visioningonward to access live links to the online resources referenced in this chapter.

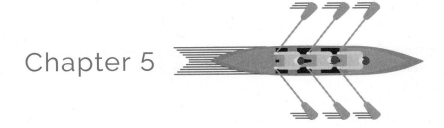

Chapter 5

VISIONING
CASE STUDY

In the education sector, we argue that it is the fundamental obligation
of organizations to make people better.

—*Doug Lemov, Erica Woolway, and Katie Yezzi (2012)*

In this chapter, Dr. Melissa (Missie) Patschke explains the visioning
process she used in two schools.

The Opening of a New School—Upper Providence
Elementary School (UPES)

In the fall, prior to the opening year of UPES, I was hired by the
Spring Ford Area School District to open a new school the following
school year. The construction of the new building was almost completed, but not a single staff member had been hired. My charge was
to interview, hire, and create an outstanding team of educators from
both internal and external applicants. In addition, I was asked to build
the vision and culture of the new school by bringing students and
families from three existing school communities together.

I knew that I wanted the new school to be a place where students,
staff, and families felt welcome, energized, and empowered to be
their best. I wanted to create a school community that was inclusive,
celebrated differences, valued individual and collective growth, as
well as found ways to have fun, play, and laugh together. I knew that

the best schools believed that with a strengths-based approach to leading and learning, all children will learn. My bottom line was that our school needed to always do what's right for kids. The details of how all of this was going to become a reality was now up to the human capital. It would take research, planning, and cultivation of a shared base of beliefs. Collective understandings would grow to become the vision of the new school.

Team Building and a Steering Team

The first and most important task was to build the team. All teachers in the school district that were appropriately certified to work in the new school were invited to apply. External postings were advertised as well. Once an interview pool was created, the interviewing began. Assisted by fellow administrators (our steering team), we hand-picked candidates who were motivated to face the challenges presented by opening a new school and who also promised to bring their best to our students each day. By the spring, every position needed for the fall was filled and in place. At this point, I started to bring groups of staff to the table to discuss needs, wants, expectations, and beliefs.

We created several committees to start the visioning work. These included but were not limited to a building advisory committee, a child study team, a pro-social committee, and a community history committee. Most importantly, we created a core-informational team that served as our steering team for the visionary work. This teacher leadership crew was composed of the school principal, counselor, nurse, psychologist, reading specialist, special educator, and a representative from each grade level in the building. Through our collective experiences, we examined what worked and what didn't work in schools during our careers. We spoke to other members of the staff and brought back ideas to add to the discussions. In addition, we delved into the latest research of the early 2000s. Critical to our consideration was early research that sparked professional learning communities and competencies. We reviewed systems theory and mental models by Peter Senge. Also, we took to heart the potential impact of Michael Fullan's change theory and implementation dip. And, finally, thought leaders such as Ronald Barth, Neila Connors, Stephen Covey, and Todd Whitaker guided our search to design a positive school culture. As our work continued, our steering team continued to meet one-on-one, in small groups with common interests, in job-alike groups, and with committees to answer questions and identify driving core values among the educators who were joining us on this adventure.

Visioning Questions for UPES

- What elements of a school contribute to a welcoming atmosphere?

- How do we empower and energize students and staff to give their best each day?

- What's important to you or to your role in a school?

- What needs to be in place to ensure that differences among us and in our students are embraced and celebrated?

- How important is it to have fun and laugh at school? How do we bring joy to our school each day?

- What does it mean from your role to do what's right for kids? How does that become our bottom line?

- What else is important for us to consider as we move forward to open a new school?

- What do we need to leave on the curb and not bring with us to the new school?

- What do we need to keep in check and revisit frequently?

As more and more answers were shared, I synthesized the responses and shared the big picture with all stakeholders. Together, we created a road map of how we, as a new school team, would interact, work, and teach. We designed a priority list for how to treat each other and how we wanted to be treated in turn. We created a vision of our core understandings that would lead to one of the best school cultures ever created. We then turned the vision into words that empowered an entire community in "kid language" to know who we are and how we operate. The following statements were the fruits of that work and are forever displayed in our school. At the end of our community meetings, we all state these beliefs together. In classrooms and in projects, we grapple with the details of what they mean to individuals and to our collective work.

Core Beliefs—The Best Children in the World Are Learning HERE!

- The Sky's the Limit at UP!

- Together, We Make a Difference! We Make It Happen!

- Upper Providence, Unbelievable Place!

- Respect and Responsibility Rock at UP!

- Believe and Succeed!

- It's All About Attitude!

As we moved ahead into the school year, we continued to meet in our identified focus groups to evaluate and measure the progress we were making in multiple areas. Each member of the steering team took monthly qualitative data from their colleagues. This was shared and tracked through reported staff perception in the areas of (1) student and parent customer service levels, (2) academic relevance and rigor, (3) staff feelings of individual value, (4) team-driven accomplishments, and (5) an overall sense of pride in school.

We charted this progress and brought the findings to the building level through monthly staff meetings. In addition, activities, programs, and points of focus were designed based on the feedback we received through this process. Eventually we added student voice and parent perception to the data to create a 360 model of feedback for the steering team.

Simultaneous to the staff vision creations, I worked with multiple stakeholders to understand the community values, the school district expectations, and the individual school beliefs. I met with individuals, small focus groups, and larger open forums. The scope of my research was as detailed as reviewing board policy, operational manuals, and base regulations and as broad as seeking to understand the heart of a community's wants, needs, and beliefs for the education and care of their children. Much of this work continued for several years after the opening of our school. The most critical thing to accomplish prior to opening was the creation of the Home & School Association.

Creating this organization from the ground up was a fascinating effort. All parents of children slated to attend the new school in the fall were invited to meet with me as early as March. A core collaborative of approximately thirty parents attended meetings. We worked through many of their ideas with the end goal of creating a supportive nonprofit organization that would allow the parents and teachers to join together in concerted efforts to support the vision of the school community. The families involved brought experiences from three different schools within the current district as well as several who had lived in other communities and were able to share those diverse experiences with the group. We spent several meetings creating the vision for this collective effort. In doing so we asked, listened, and answered several key questions.

Key Questions for Parents

- What are the important components you want to see in your child's elementary school?

- How do you want your child to feel about his or her school experience?

- What is the role of a parent–teacher association? What isn't the role of this group?

- What types of activities have you experienced in the past that were positive contributions to your child's elementary school? Which did your children enjoy the most and why?

- What types of fund-raisers did you find successful at previous schools?

- How have you seen volunteerism be positively generated in other schools?

- What are your ideas to ensure we have a diversity of parents involved in the organization?

- What type of leadership should be created to guide this group?

- What else is important for us to consider as we create and then operate a parent–teacher group for UPE?

As we worked with this impact group, I shared findings of what worked and what didn't work at schools that were known to some in our circle as well as those featured in state and national publications. At the time, NAESP, ASCD, and National School Development Council (NSDC) had current publications featuring schools that work, how to improve schools, and schools we want. Many of these documents were shared with stakeholders for discussion and consideration. Through this review of current research, parents and community members were able to express what they wanted for their children and, in turn, what they did not want to see in their community elementary school. Ideas that were expressed included but were not limited to parents wanting the following for their children and themselves:

- To be safe, happy, and loved

- To feel welcomed, wanted, and valued as parents in the school

- Master teachers and staff who make our children their priority

- A school that supports and values changing families and diversity in the community

- Strong and clear communications between home and school

- Opportunities to get involved with the educational program

- Relevant and rigorous foundational academic curriculum

- Opportunities to build a sense of contribution to the community

As the opening of the school approached, much of this work was in place. It's important to note that a significant amount of vision making is embedded in the daily work. Making what you focus on match your collective beliefs is the aspect that truly steers a vision into a genuine place of value to the group. From that point on, everything begins to grow and build. There is a fluid nature to visions. They are not fixed. Just as human beings change, so do systems. Visions must too have the pliability required to move forward and shift to fit positive growth. When the vision is owned by the majority of stakeholders, the acceleration of teamwork, trust, and organizational synergy happens.

Thirteen Years Later—Refreshing Our Vision

As years progressed, staff were added, and others moved on. Students and families passed through the hallways and became alumni cohorts. We tapped this amazing resource and recycled our teen alumni into high school helpers for our classrooms. This reconnection allowed us to sustain amazing relationships but also supported our current students with great role models in their community. UPES had grown "up" and into an amazing culture. As relationships continued to move forward, student achievement and collective efficacy was on a path of certain success.

As part of a yearly conversation with individual staff members, we would discuss their growth, ambitions, and future focus for their classrooms and their careers. About thirteen years into our school journey, I shifted these isolated talks into small focus groups. My intention was to refresh and recharge our school's vision. It was time to examine where we were, what was important to us, and where we were headed. I divided the school staff into small, intentionally diverse groups. I called these groups *staf-faculty* focus groups, a combination of staff and faculty. I made sure that each team was comprised with relational dynamics that would allow a voice for all. I shuffled roles and positions. I also was intentional with cross dynamics and alternating perspectives. It was important not only for me to hear the conversation but for staff to hear each other's perspectives on several important topics. In addition, I also met with job-alike groups to explore additional resources, needs, and wants from department, duty, or teaching assignment areas.

Staf-faculty Focus Group Questions

- Describe where we are right now as a school community.

- Where do I want our school to be?

- In what areas do we need to grow or change?

- What do we value and not want to lose focus on?

- What do I do to relieve stress and focus on my own health?

- What am I doing that I can realistically make less of a professional priority?

You'll notice from the questions that the last two are unique. Stress in education is a real hazard to a school community. Often, the personality traits that make amazing teachers also make it difficult to let go. My purpose of talking in focus groups about the upkeep of our health and letting something go was to make the expectation real. When teachers hear from their colleagues and leaders the importance of taking care of themselves and that they can't possibly do it all, it makes a difference. My expectation is that they take care of themselves and their families so that they can be the best people for our students. This underlying message needs to be in the foundation of all that you create in a school. Staff need to know you care and value them as well as those they love. Once that belief is there, you'll find no visible end to their commitment.

After the data were collected from all the small groups, we came together as a school community. I shared the collective data across several meetings. We spent time talking about what's important to us, what we have grown to cherish, and what we need to let go of. These conversations became personal to many of the staff. We did this work over three months, ending the school year with several strong common visions of how to move forward as a school community.

As a response to this work, our school team created the UPE 5 as the core belief system for our school culture. These are five beliefs that drive how anyone in our school interacts with each other as well as holds themselves to the bar of expectations. This vision is shared by every student, staff member, and visitor to our school. We all say the Pro-Social Pledge in the morning right after the Pledge of Allegiance. This communal message emphasizes the UPE 5. Adults make the commitment to our students to follow the UPE 5, and in turn our students commit to the same expectations. The UPE 5 has facilitated common language and unified expectations for the vision of our school culture.

UPE 5

1. I will keep myself and others safe.
2. I will keep my comments positive and encouraging.
3. I will be honest. I will give and receive kind feedback.
4. I will focus on what's important.
5. I will always participate to the best of my ability.

Pro-Social Pledge

Today, I will do my best!

> I will keep myself and others safe.
>
> I will keep my comments positive and encouraging.
>
> I will be honest. I will give and receive kind feedback.
>
> I will focus on what's important.
>
> I will always participate to the best of my ability.
>
> I can learn.
>
> I will learn!
>
> You see, I know it's all up to me!

In addition, this refresh of the UPES vision was a positive experience for everyone involved. Staff were able to enjoy all that's right in our school. Individuals knew that their voices were heard. Ideas were sparked, and new paths were forged. Most importantly, the elements in our school that grew to become characteristics of greatness or historic sacred rituals were identified and discussed. Perspectives were heard. If the item was positive, it was celebrated. If there were concerns surrounding a practice, it was minimized or discarded. The new vision moving forward was owned by those in the present. The refresh was exciting. Having gone through this as a leader, I would never wait thirteen years to engage in this process again. I wish I had done the refresh before year ten. Having said that, we will be revisiting a vision refresh soon.

An Existing School With New Leadership at Spring City Elementary School

Over the summer months, prior to the start of a new school year, I was asked to provide leadership to an additional school in our district. This was a school similar to UPES but much smaller in population, and it operated on a hybrid technology instructional philosophy. As an experienced leader entering a new community, I knew there was so much to learn. Before I was able to work on a vision for this school, I needed to learn the history, the players, and the current philosophies. I started this work by meeting individually with every person who worked at the school. Mrs. Choi, the school's newly appointed head teacher, and I carved out time to conduct this research.

Spring City Staff Entry Plan Questions

- What do you love most about the work you do?

- What has been a highlight of something that you accomplished last year?

- What are your biggest hurdles at work?

- How can we support you as you try to overcome these hurdles?

- What do you need from me as your school principal?

- What's our biggest obstacle as a school?

- What do you feel is an "elephant in the room" that we should be aware of? How do you think we all can address the concern?

- How do you best use your talents at work?

- How can we help you use your strengths even more at school?

- Is there anything else that we don't know to even ask that you feel is important for us to know as we start the school year?

We also met with key leaders of the parent community. We asked this group questions about how they saw their child's school, what the strengths were, and where they wanted to see improvements. While we listened, questioned, and sought to understand the culture, the community, and the vision of this existing school, it became clear to us that there were some strong underlying values that supported the work happening on a daily basis. The school community held a deep pride in the small, private feel in the school culture. Every adult knew every child by name. Every employee, no matter their role, was important and affected kids daily. Parents were supportive of the school, and the local community saw the school as a hub of the town. Having been in existence since 1957, most everyone in the small town who had lived their lives in Spring City had also attended Spring City Elementary. The heartstrings of this little blue-collar area tethered around the children, their homes, and a strong sense of community pride.

As we embarked on the new school year, I shared the general findings with the staff. There were things they cherished and things they needed to let go. There were items to improve and elements that deserved to be celebrated. We started to create a shared vision. Proudly, the one thing that we all agreed on was to do what's right for the kids. Everything else is under construction. I'm halfway through the first year of leading this new school. Already, I can see that the collective vision is one of excellence, pride, and perseverance. This school family wants the best for their children and is willing to give what it takes to achieve that end. I see newly sparked passion in teachers and unconditional love in the hearts of parents. As we progress into the second half of the year, we'll be answering some key questions together as a school. In the end, I'm sure we will develop the forward moving vision of "a little school that could."

Vision Questions for Spring City Staff

- What do we believe about teaching and learning?
- What's it like to be a student in our school?
- What's it like to be a parent of a student in our school?
- What do we know works best for our kids?
- What do we want to see in the future for this school?
- What do we have today that we don't want to let go?
- What do we need to let go or refurbish to be able to move forward?
- How do you best take care of yourself and your health?
- In what ways do your colleagues help you the most?
- Do the words on our website match who we are as a community?
- What should they say?

Conclusions—Collaboration Is Key

Missie shared her visioning experience across two schools and more than thirteen years in suburban Pennsylvania. She highlighted the importance of working together to build a vision for your school that includes everyone's point of view. She gave us examples of questions to ask parents and staf-faculty when you convene meetings of each group. She also shared her succinct, action-driven vision statements for UPES and Spring City Elementary School, which are excellent examples of visions that inspire stakeholders to get behind them. Without a supportive team, your vision will be just that: only *your* vision. We hope Missie's experience has inspired you to collaborate with your school community so that everyone feels your school's vision is *theirs*.

Practical Points to Ponder

- Vision work is a community job. When staff, faculty, parents, and other stakeholders want to see the school you envision, you'll have a lot of help to make it a reality. How can you engage administrators, teachers, staff, parents, and other stakeholders in your vision work from the first stages?

- Everyone's voice is important, but you'll need a steering team of two or three people to drive the change. Who first comes to mind for this role? Who might be a good fit for this role? Who might not seem an obvious choice?

- Our modern world changes rapidly. We will discuss in Chapter 8 how to create a forward-thinking vision, but even then, visions need revisions. How often will you check with your school community to make sure your vision is still relevant for your building, district, and world?

In Chapter 5, we examined an exemplar case study of one school leader who used what we believe is *a* best practice for visioning. Visioning is not one size fits all, but the systems and change theory thinking, iterative planning, and collaborative nature of Principal Patschke's visioning work at UPES and Spring City Elementary School is an excellent example of how these elements of the process can come together to create lasting change in a school. We encourage you to take away the aspects of Missie's process that would work best for your school.

Ideas for Leading and Learning

- Visioning is not a quick process. Before leaders engage their community, engaging in thoughtful reflection, in-depth research, and opinion gathering will better support their efforts. How have you reflected on your school's needs? Have you explored Peter Senge's systems thinking, Michael Fullan's change theory, or the work of other educational thought leaders like Ronald Barth, Neila Connors, Stephen Covey, and Todd Whitaker?

- In a school or district, change often starts from the top, but a more successful change often comes when those in charge (administrators, superintendents, and other school leaders) listen to the voices on the ground (students, teachers, and parents). What's your plan to engage multiple voices in the visioning process from the beginning? How will you communicate with your community? How often will you meet? When and where will you meet?

- One reason Principal Patschke believes her vision was successful is that parents bought into it from the beginning because she involved them in the process from day one. Each school and district has unique challenges with parent populations. What are the barriers to forming a healthy and effective working relationship with the parents in your community? How can you get parents excited to engage in this work with you?

Resources to Explore

Scan the QR Code or visit https://resources.corwin.com/visioningonward to access live links to this book's online resources.

Chapter 6

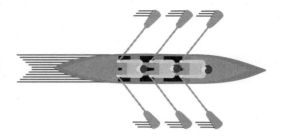

VISIONING STEPS 5–8

If we have the courage to revolutionize education, our children will find their strengths, create fulfilling paths forward, and attack the many problems we are dumping on their laps.

—*Ted Dintersmith (2018)*

We presented the initial four steps for visioning in schools and school districts in Chapter 4. These included the following:

Step 1—*Form a vision steering team,* and develop a blueprint for your visioning process.

Step 2—*Determine who will be involved in visioning.* Consider community stakeholders, parents, teachers, school staff, and maybe even students. Consider how to allow all voices to be heard *by each other*, not just the decision makers or administrators.

Step 3—*Develop your first draft* of your vision. Imagine your school the way you would like it to be.

Step 4—*Research exemplars and options.*

That chapter also included examples of visions for green schools, schools that are safe and supportive, schools with personalized instruction, schools that infuse technology or music throughout the school day and school environment, STEM schools, and schools furthering learning through applying neuroscientific principles.

In Chapter 5, Missie shared how she implemented this visioning process in two schools in Pennsylvania. She not only shared her process but included a statement of the core beliefs and values of one of her current schools. In her process of developing a vision, Missie involved a wide group of school and community stakeholders over a period of several years. The vision for her first school was supported by research from scholars such as Peter Senge and Michael Fullan and from thought leaders such as Ronald Barth, Neila Connors, Stephen Covey, and Todd Whitaker.

Steps 5–8

Figure 6.1 shows the next four visioning steps:

Step 5—*Refine your vision using an iterative visioning process.*

Step 6—*Develop your mission and goal statements, and determine how to measure progress.*

Step 7—*Secure consensus.* Ensure that you are communicating with those who didn't participate or who have a different vision.

Step 8—*Develop an action plan to implement your vision.*

Figure 6.1   Visioning Process—Steps 5–8

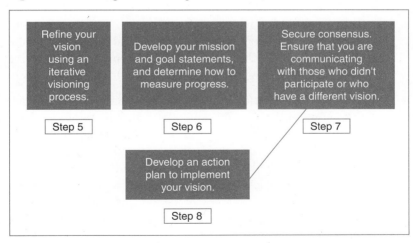

Step 5—Refine Your Vision Using an Iterative Visioning Process

Return for a minute to your notes on the first step of the visioning process, and examine the vision you developed for your school or district. Look at the vision statement you developed, and compare it to what you and your team learned as they researched exemplars and options.

To guide you through the process of revising or enhancing your vision statement, return to your notes on exemplars, examine Key Learning 4.8 and the extended researching options exercise in Chapter 4, and answer the following questions:

> What was particularly notable about the exemplars you identified?
>
> How did your vision statement compare to the exemplars?
>
> Based on what you observed, how might you modify your vision?

These review and reflection activities can be conducted with a small, core learning team or with the larger community. Sometimes it works well to start with a small team and then hold a session with a larger group. If that is the option, you might consider a process whereby the following occurs:

- Team members agree to represent each of the three or four exemplars that seemed to be most appealing. A few of the team members each have five to seven minutes to describe what was appealing about the exemplars to the larger group.

- Participants divide up into four or five small groups and discuss how the Exemplars have affected their thinking about the vision for their school or district. Each group may opt to modify your school's vision based on the exemplar. From this process, members write the modified vision on a piece of chart paper. These are shared with the larger group. Members could be responsible for taking alternative visions to students and families to continue the visioning process with more of their input.

- In the case study in Chapter 5, Missie described core beliefs. These became slogans that helped finalize the vision. The core beliefs at her school included phrases such as these: "The Best Children in the World Are Learning HERE! The Sky's the Limit at UP! Together, We Make a Difference! We Make It Happen!" At your school or district, slogans could be generated by teachers, students, and families and could be used as a part of arriving at the final vision statement.

After a couple of weeks, a visioning team can meet again to review slogans and alternative vision statements, and if needed, a nominal voting process can be used to arrive at the best vision. With nominal voting, each member is given two dots—perhaps one red and one blue. The red dot is used to vote for the first choice and the blue one for the second choice.

After viewing the results, revise your vision.

Over the next few weeks, live with the new vision. You might want to consider posting it in a few places, holding discussions with students and families, and then meeting again, reviewing comments, checking to see if improvements are needed, and arriving at the final vision.

Step 6—Develop Mission and Goal Statements, and Determine How to Measure Progress

According to Kaplan, Norton, and Barrows (2008), "a mission statement is a brief, typically one-sentence, statement that defines the fundamental purpose of the organization" (p. 3).

Mission Statements and the Strategic Planning Process

A well-communicated mission statement unites school and district leadership, teachers, families, students, and other stakeholders. A mission statement sits within a larger cycle of strategy and planning, which includes the following:

- Developing a mission statement in collaboration with the faculty and staff

- Using the mission statement to develop strategic goals and performance targets

- Developing a strategic plan and initiatives in service of that plan

- Implementing the strategic plan and associated initiatives

- Evaluating success by comparing performance outcomes to targets

- Revising strategic goals, performance targets, and strategic plans

The strategic planning cycle is continuous and ongoing. Districts set goals and performance targets, evaluate progress against performance targets, and regularly refine goals and targets. Although performance targets are generally reviewed and revised at least annually, mission statements are broader and more enduring.

How Important Is a School's Mission Statement?

The College Board developed a program called EXCELerator in 2009 to assess and improve college readiness in high schools. In 2009, EXCELerator staff gathered data on goal setting and mission statements and found that districts with mission statements aligned to college readiness showed "pervasive commitment and consensus around college readiness throughout the entire district community, from district leaders to school leaders and staff and among community stakeholders" (College Board, 2011). EXCELerator staff reported:

- School staff commitment to college readiness was inconsistent unless districts also had a college readiness mission statement.

- "Districts with mission statements clearly aligned to college readiness, but lacking goals and strategy, struggled to move towards college readiness" (p.3).

Shelley Habegger (2008), an educational consultant in Ohio, found from her study of principals in highly effective schools serving low socioeconomic areas that the most important goal was to "develop positive relationships." Mission statements at these schools were the "guiding force" for decision-making (p. 45). In one school, the principal read the mission statement as part of the daily morning announcement.

Both inside and outside the school, a mission statement is the marketing tool people are most likely to encounter and remember. The mission statement has to tell both parents and faculty why the school exists, what the school's purpose is, and what the school intends to achieve. According to Les Stein's 2016 article "Schools Need Leaders—Not Managers," a school's mission statement should be: (1) short, concise, and to the point; (2) meaningful to all of its stakeholders; (3) realistic and implementable; and (4) measurable. Although Stein describes the desirability of being able to quantify progress toward reaching one's mission, many schools separate the quantitative component and include it in goal statements.

An Example of a Successful Mission Statement

The Don Watson Academy, a residential and day school serving students with social emotional disabilities, ages 6–18 in Lancaster, Massachusetts, embraces the individuality of each student through trauma-informed care. A part of the RFK Children's Action Corp (n.d.), its mission statement fosters individual well-being:

> Don Watson Academy is dedicated to the growth and learning of students by providing a safe, therapeutic environment that enhances the quality of life of each individual.
>
> As educators, we encourage the students to replace negative behaviors with positive actions. We foster personal and social growth where excellence in individual achievement is valued and respected.

This mission statement meets all of Stein's criteria (see Online Resource 6.1). It is concisely worded and relevant to everyone at the school; its stated goals are reasonable, and their success can be measured, even if the specific quantitative criteria are not explicitly stated as part of the mission statement.

Return to your vision statement. Using Stein's criteria, draft a mission statement to support your vision.

Your Mission Statement

Insert your draft mission statement here:

Now review in light of Stein's criteria. Does it meet the following criteria:

☐ 1. Short, concise, and to the point?

☐ 2. Meaningful to all of its stakeholders?

☐ 3. Realistic and implementable?

☐ 4. Measurable?

Leithwood, Harris, and Hopkins (2008), in reporting the results of a synthesis of the evidence of effective leadership practices, report that together, building visions and setting directions are one of four critical factors. Expounding upon their results, Leithwood and his colleagues conclude that building a vision and setting directions are "about establishment of shared purpose as a stimulant to one's work" (p. 30).

Key Learning 6.1

Your Mission as a Stimulant to Your Work

Review your draft mission statement one more time—how does it become a "stimulant to the work" at your school? For example, does it help set the stage for expectations for school climate, teacher–pupil interaction, communications with families, or academic achievement?

In the space below, write an explanation of how your draft mission serves as a catalyst for the programs and initiatives of your school or district.

Goals

Once you have agreement on your school's or district's vision and mission, the process of setting goals that support your mission comes next. Collaborative school leadership is furthered by goal setting (DuFour & Marzano, 2011; Hallinger & Heck, 2010; Supovitz, Sirinides, & May, 2010).

Effective communication of the school's mission and fostering high, but attainable, school goals is another factor associated with student success (Nettles & Herrington, 2007).

Vivianne Robinson, a professor in New Zealand, in a meta-analysis of the effect sizes (EF) of leadership components with student outcomes in a review of international studies between 1978 and 2006, found a small effect size (average EF = .35) of schoolwide goal setting. In describing the importance of a coherent program, she concluded that

> goal-setting increases performance and learning. It also has positive psychological consequences by providing a sense of priority and purpose and thus solving the problem of everything feeling equally important and overwhelming. This increased focus and sense of purpose increases enjoyment of tasks and willingness to take on challenges.
>
> (Robinson, Hohepa, & Lloyd, 2007, p. 11)

In a 2015 study of organizational statements in schools, Gurley, Peters, Collins, & Fifolt define a goal statement as a tool for educators to "spell out precisely what level of performance is to be achieved in the selected domain (e.g., student learning, professional development) and what steps are to be taken, by whom, in order to achieve the goal" (p. 16). According to *District Leadership that Works,* a book by Robert Marzano and Timothy Waters (2009), there are five actions in which district leaders should engage:

1. Ensuring collaborative goal setting
2. Establishing nonnegotiable goals for achievement and instruction
3. Creating board alignment with and support of district goals
4. Monitoring achievement and instructional goals
5. Allocating resources to support goals for achievement and instruction

Gurley et al. (2015) agree with Manzano and Waters, noting that in the current culture of "increased accountability for student learning and professional practice, setting clear, measurable performance goals has become common practice for school leaders" (p. 224).

Key Learning 6.2

Identify Four or Five Goals for Your School or District

1.

2.

3.

4.

5.

Measuring Progress

Hanover Research (2014), in its description of best practices in school improvement planning, concludes that school improvement planning is only worthwhile if collected data and resulting conclusions are repeatedly acted upon. When you are developing your action plan, which we describe in Step 8, make sure that you are developing a system of accountability that measures your progress toward your goals. This means that your goals should be measurable. Keep this in mind as you develop them. We'll go into more detail later in this chapter.

Step 7—Secure Consensus. Ensure That You Are Communicating With Those Who Didn't Participate or Who Have a Different Vision

An important step in adopting and beginning to actualize a vision is to make sure to reach out to those key stakeholders in your school or district who were not directly involved in setting your vision. Tension can develop when people are left out of the loop or when adequate time is not taken to help them reflect on the rationale for your vision and your hopes and dreams for working toward that vision.

There are many options for how to communicate with those outside the visioning process. Choose which method works best for your school or district:

- Announcement in school or district newsletters inviting responses via e-mail

- Town-hall style meetings for all community members

- Letters or flyers sent to all families and other invested stakeholders

- Explanation on the school or district website with a comment section

- Informal meetings in appropriate settings

On a similar note, sometimes stakeholders (educators, parents, families, and community members) may hold different visions. School leaders are advised to use formal and informal means to dialogue about the differing visions and how to move forward in light of the differences. Sometimes these differences can be bridged, perhaps even through reaching some compromises and considering how to allocate some resources for the competing visions. When moving forward in implementation of a plan to reach a vision, key participants may find themselves in a bit of an upheaval. For example, if your school has had an emphasis on reading and math literacy, and wants to move toward implementing a STEM/STEAM agenda, teachers may need professional development about how to integrate engineering principles into their instruction. Schools may also find that they will move towards a STEM curriculum that includes a considerable emphasis on hands-on, project-based instruction. This may be an uncomfortable move for some of the teachers. In these instances, some teachers or other staff may be more comfortable transferring to another school with a vision and mission that are more consistent with their experience and expertise.

Step 8—Develop an Action Plan to Implement Your Vision

Without an action plan, the talents of your diverse steering team and staf-faculty voices will have no direction and may be squandered.

The School Improvement Network, an organization that has helped more than 20,000 schools make changes that resulted in improved student outcomes, warns that if your plan does not consist of actionable steps, you might hit a roadblock (Pipkin, 2015). Although goals and mission statements are essential to ensuring that everyone in a school or district is on the same page, you'll never reach those goals unless you take the time to determine what steps of action will lead your school or district from where you are to where you want to be and which steps will be assigned to each person in your educational community.

How to Develop an Action Plan

1. *Work backward from your goals and mission statement* to determine what steps you need to take to go from where you are to where you want to be. Look back at your needs assessment to inform this process (see Steps 2 and 3 in Chapter 4).

When you're envisioning where you want your school or district to be, it can be overwhelming to think about moving from where you are to where you want to be in just one school year. But there are so many small goals that you can accomplish along the way. You know your school's or district's growth areas from the needs assessment you did in Step 3. You've already researched exemplars and examples in Step 4. Revisit what these schools did to identify what kind of policy shifts, new protocols, interventions, programs, curriculums, and other tools you can bring to your school to reach your goals.

2. *Break down your steps to be as simple and actionable as possible.*

To reach your goals, you can't expect to make only one or two changes. Transforming your educational community is going to take complex steps that are actually made up of several steps within a step. For example, you wouldn't expect your school to improve its reading proficiency rates from 28 to 85 percent by simply stating that you will implement a new reading program. Getting an entire school or district to use a new reading program encompasses more than one step. Who is going to choose the program? Where is funding for this program and related materials coming from? When and how are teachers going to receive training on the program? When will you roll out the new program? Will you start in one school, grade level, or classroom and expand it or do a district- or schoolwide roll out?

Look at each of the steps you determined you need to take to work toward your goal and break it down into all the sub-steps they involve. You can utilize your steering team or create new teams to tackle each larger step. Ask your team to think of all the questions that might come up as you try to implement that step and create a sub-step that requires action to answer each question. For the example if implementing a new reading program district-wide, actionable sub-steps might look like this:

- Form a committee to choose an appropriate reading curriculum.

- Compile a list of evidence-based reading programs.

- Research different evidence-based reading programs.

- Determine which reading program fits our district's needs best.

- Reserve space and time to train teachers on the new program.

- Communicate this change to parents, guardians, and other necessary stakeholders.

- Check in with teachers about how well the program is working for them.

- Assess the success of the program at the end of the school year.

A great way to ensure that your steps are actionable is to start each step with an action verb. Notice that each of these steps requires *someone to do something.*

3. *Determine whose responsibility each action step would be.*

Now that you have an idea of what needs to get done to reach your goals, it's time to decide who is going to do what. You have a diverse team of staff and faculty with a variety of experiences and skills. Be mindful of which staff members' talents would be used most effectively for which steps. It might be tempting to assign entire grade teams or subject teams to certain steps in your action plan, but look more closely at the actionable sub-steps to see if there might be someone else in the school with a unique point of view or some valuable experience with that subject matter that's not on the team that first came to mind.

If we look back at our sub-steps, for example, a team of each school's reading specialists might be the obvious choice to form a districtwide committee to choose a reading curriculum, but a more robust committee might be composed of a selection of reading specialists from the top- and bottom-performing schools, a group of English language arts teachers from different schools and grade levels, a special education teacher, a gifted education teacher, and faculty outside of English language arts so that you're gathering opinions from a variety of perspectives.

Analyze each action sub-step, and consult with other administrators about who might be the best fit for each step. If you don't know who has the expertise needed to complete a sub-step, utilize your network of educators to find out who might be a good fit. Don't forget to make a record of who has been assigned which step.

4. *Create a system of accountability with indicators of who has responsibility, what is to be achieved, and the proposed deadlines.*

Using shared spreadsheets on Google Docs or shared project management sites like Trello and Basecamp (visit **Online Resources 6.2** and **6.3**) are great ways to achieve transparency and accountability. You can decide to leave comments on or off so that team members can give each other feedback and encouragement on progress. Make sure your deadlines are realistic but that they push you and your team to put in the hard work visioning takes to meet your goals in a timely manner.

When you are creating your system of accountability, whether it's online, on a poster in the teacher's lounge, or in a notebook you carry around to team meetings, make sure that when you write out each person's responsibilities, you are as detailed as possible so there is no confusion as to what each person has been asked to do and when they are expected to do it. "Create a five-minute PowerPoint presentation explaining the differences between the reading groups you researched, your suggestions, and a rationale by May 31," will yield much more effective results than "Research different reading groups."

5. *Clearly communicate each person's role to the entire group.*

If your accountability system is shared via an online platform, be sure that everyone's roles and responsibilities are clearly posted in a central location like the first sheet of a Google Sheet or the HQ of your school's Visioning Basecamp. Everyone should be able to quickly look at a chart and see who to go to if they have questions or opinions to share about a certain aspect of the visioning process. If your school prefers paper communication, make sure to create a document that you pass out to all school staff and faculty.

Roles often shift as the visioning process begins and educators realize that they have strong opinions about some aspect of the process they didn't expect to light such a fire. Be sure to communicate changes in roles as soon as possible and as widely as possible. When these roles are in an editable place online, this task is much simpler as you can set up e-mail alerts to message everyone when a change is made.

6. *Have regular check-ins to see if your action plan is effective for everyone.*

Just because you think your action plan is working doesn't mean that it's working for everyone. Even the best-intentioned plans have unintended consequences. Perhaps you're converting a rarely used space into a book nook to encourage reading, but you didn't realize that some of the paraeducators liked to use that space to chat during breaks because it's nice and quiet. If you're not talking to as many people as possible in the school throughout this process, you may find at the end that some people who seemed on board had a problem from day one.

It's impossible to make everyone happy, and you should try to find the balance between what will do the most good for your students and what will make the most people happy. When someone doesn't like your plan, keep asking questions to figure out what exactly they want. With this example, simply finding another small corner, perhaps at the back of the library or in a classroom empty that period, for the paraeducators to chat during their breaks could gain you a whole faction of supporters who might otherwise detract from your vision.

Conclusions—Developing an Action Plan as a Team

The second half of the visioning process that we presented in this chapter asks you to look at your school community and work together to design your vision mindfully. You and a smaller team may have drafted a first attempt at a vision, but listen to the voices of the stakeholders in your school community to arrive at a vision that fits everyone's needs. Revisit the needs assessment discussed in Chapter 4 during this process as you see fit. After completing the iterative visioning process, craft mission and goal statements that are measurable. Before committing to these statements, consult members of the community who weren't involved in previous stages of this process or who had differing opinions and find compromises that meet most people's needs. The last step is to develop an action plan that clearly defines everyone's roles in the transformation process, deadlines, and measures of progress.

Practical Points to Ponder

- We have emphasized teamwork. What steps can you take to ensure that you have effective teams?
- How will you use available technologies to enhance your visioning process?
- How will you measure progress toward your goals? Is this likely to be an efficient and effective process?

For-profit companies have built-in parameters for measuring progress—their finances are their bottom line. Schools, on the other hand, like many other nonprofit agencies, are most concerned with their impact on their stakeholders. Implementing goals and action plans is time-consuming, so leaders are cautioned to ensure that there are adequate opportunities to celebrate progress and to share successes—both of which are part of an effective approach to community building.

Ideas for Leading and Learning

- Somewhere along the way as you are implementing your action plan, life will interfere—new priorities will emerge—and you and your team may feel stretched or even frustrated. What can you do to guard from being derailed?

- Consider visioning from the perspective of someone at your school or district who is not completely sold on your vision. What can you do to enhance participation from that person(s)?

- As you measure progress, you may find that there is room for improvement. What kinds of actions or activities might you use to expedite your progress?

Resources to Explore

Scan the QR Code or visit https://resources.corwin.com/visioningonward to access live links to the online resources referenced in this chapter.

Chapter 7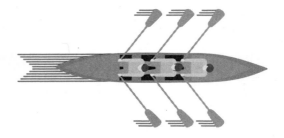

BARRIERS AND SUSTAINABILITY

> Vision is not enough. It must be combined with venture. It is not
> enough to stare up the steps, we must step up the stairs.
>
> —*Vaclav Havel*

Visioning is not always a walk in a park. Sometimes it can be more like climbing a mountain or stumbling down a path as you strive to gain footing. Similar to preparing for an extended hike on the Appalachian or Pacific Crest Trails, principals will be better positioned to embark on their own visioning journeys after having first taken the time to learn from the experience of others—mapping out their own course before beginning. In many ways, visioning can be likened to the process of blazing a trail: chopping down trees, removing boulders, and clearing brush to create a new path. This chapter will help prepare readers for their journeys by sharing some of the challenges principals and other school leaders faced as they reconsidered the role of their schools within their districts, led ongoing negotiations with district-level administrators, and built consensus within their school communities.

Vision, Mission, and Goals—Implementation

Schools are well versed in implementing new plans, and often, once goals and action plans have been developed, teams within schools will begin activities to move the school along the path of achieving objectives and accomplishing goals. During this phase, leaders will want to make sure that the new vision and mission are infused into the school culture. This might include the following:

Tips on How to Infuse Your Vision Into School Culture

- Make the vision visible: hoist banners; use symbols (perhaps a new logo) to represent the vision. Have students participate in developing posters or writing essays about the new vision.

- Set aside time for team planning.

- Use the school's website and social media to keep the vision and mission up front and center.

- Provide professional development and learning opportunities for staff and students.

- Consider the impact of the new vision and mission across the board (curriculum, routines, policies, and activities with families and the community).

- Conduct a special event (a kick-off, a forum, or a discussion).

- Invite the local newspapers and TV stations to the school.

- Monitor progress and problem-solving.

During the first few months, it will be particularly important to dialogue with stakeholders who may not have been involved in developing the vision or may be reticent to embrace it. However, much of the action should be with the early adopters—the strongest supporters—to take advantage of the momentum and the mandate for change.

Lead the Visioning Journey

During the first stages of implementation, leaders need to demonstrate their capacity to be captains of their ships, leading their crews through storms on the high seas. When leading the process, leaders will count on a climate of trust and a sense of loyalty as the group identifies what will come next for the greater good of an organization, its members, and its stakeholders.

When exacting change through visioning, it's imperative that the approach is systematic and thorough (Gleeson, 2018). Exacting change requires building consensus and engagement at every level of an organization. The first step is getting everyone all in. When looked at on the whole, this may seem like an overwhelming and daunting task. As we look closer, though, there are resources and methods outside the confines of our institutions that can guide us through this process:

- Clearly articulate the changes needed across the organization and community.

- Involve as many stakeholders as possible, and give them a forum to voice their opinions.

- Emotionally connect with stakeholders, and make them feel valued and heard.

- Proactively manage fear, fatigue, and conflict, and address them head-on when they arise.

- Celebrate successes—including the little ones!

- Don't be afraid to admit mistakes and tweak your vision based on feedback or new developments.

Key Learning 7.1

Leading the Visioning Journey

How will you communicate changes with your organization and community?

Which stakeholders can you involve?

How will you make stakeholders feel like a valued part of this process?

How will you address fear, fatigue, and conflict?

How will you celebrate big and little successes?

As the race begins, we can define our vision through these supports and get our teams to the finish line by building consensus and relying on sustained commitment. As we proceed, it is important to realize that communication is an ongoing need, and leaders are called upon to continuously inspire, even as they go about their daily business. A clear, inspirational message that is succinct and powerful can continue to drive implementation even as doubts are voiced and support slides.

Obstacles on the Path

Even as you take a few deep breaths once you have arrived at a vision for your school, more challenges remain. Here are a few things that change agents report as part of the ongoing battle to move the needle forward:

- Some people who have doubts keep quiet until you are ready to move forward.
- Life interferes.
- Prices go up.
- Budgets are cut, or resources are reallocated.
- Districts or schools are confronted with competing agendas.
- Leadership changes, and you have to renew buy-in.
- New priorities arise and take precedence.
- Poor communication leads to misunderstandings and confusion.
- Apathy sets in as the inspiration or motivation disappears.
- Conflict arises, and hard-fought consensus breaks down.
- Outside resistance to change flares up.

(Airasian, 1989; Alsher, 2015)

Throughout this process there will be many ups and downs. As a leader and change agent, you need to remain committed and courageous. Remind yourself of what you're working to accomplish and why it matters. Build relationships, and rely on others to help you along the way. Encourage and support each other, and hold yourselves accountable. Keep the four stages of change in mind, and focus on what you as a leader should be doing during each stage to best support the team and move everyone forward. Barriers and challenges will arise, but together you can accomplish more than you can imagine.

One way to handle barriers is to use a system of Force Field Analysis. Force Field Analysis was created by Kurt Lewin in the 1940s for social psychology work (Lewin, 1946). Now, it is often used in business to reason through and execute tough decisions (see Figure 7.1).

Force Field Analysis helps people analyze forces working for and against change. For change to happen, the driving forces must be strengthened and/or the resisting forces weakened.

To use Force Field Analysis, define your goal or vision for change. Then think about the forces that help drive that change, such as poor educational outcomes, declining teacher morale, and

Figure 7.1   Force Field Analysis

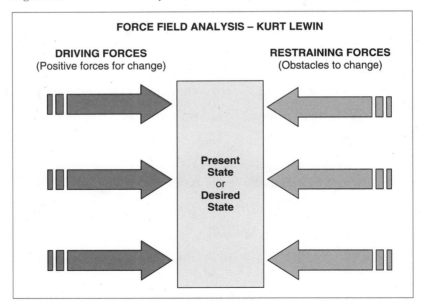

changing demographic trends. Consider the following questions to help identify change-influencing forces:

- What educational benefit will the change deliver?
- Who supports the change? Who is against it? Why?
- Do you have the resources to make the change work?
- What costs and risks are involved?

What Processes Will Be Affected?

Then, think about the forces that will impede change, such as fears of the unknown, existing organizational structures, or government legislation. Next, assign values from one (weak) to five (strong) based on the importance of each factor. Analyze how the forces for and against change compare, and think about how you might amplify supportive forces and weaken resistive forces (MindTools Content Team, n.d.).

Challenges in Implementing Heart Centered Learning

Dr. Christine Mason encountered many challenges in implementing her vision for Heart Centered Learning® over a period of ten years with teams of educators. One of the barriers was competing visions of social emotional learning or trauma-informed care that arose from much larger and more powerful organizations. Another barrier was a lack of commitment from larger organizations that initially appeared interested but never became fully engaged in supporting our vision. However, by 2019, the term *Heart Centered Learning* was becoming more important to the field of education as schools are striving to become more trauma-informed. In addressing the challenges over a period of years, here are some steps that Dr. Mason and CEI took to promote their vision and gain greater acceptance and adoption. What follows is a list of implementation strategies CEI used that you might also adapt for your own implementation initiatives.

Promoting Heart Centered Learning

- Hold focus groups and presentations on Heart Centered Learning at national meetings.

- Develop a monthly enewsletter, and used the term *Heart Centered Learning* repeatedly in that enewsletter and blog posts.

- Use social media (including Facebook, LinkedIn, and Twitter) to disseminate information about Heart Centered Learning.

- Acknowledge educators who were supporting CEI's plans.

- Keep track of competing visions to understand which visions show promise to increase our understanding of the response of the educator, to continue to compare our vision, and as appropriate, to take steps to differentiate our work from others.

- Write books that explicate aspects of Heart Centered Learning.

- Fund pilot implementation and direct a New England Childhood-Trauma Learning Collaborative to increase visibility and use of the proposed Heart Centered Learning steps. Pilot studying and forming teams, alliances, or membership groups can all boost visibility and provide greater insight on how to implement specific practices.

- Seek external funding, and collaborate with other researchers to investigate Heart Centered Learning.

- Develop an instrument S-CCATE (see Chapter 8) to help track implementation of Heart Centered Learning.

- Participate in competitions and gain recognition from the Ashoka Foundation as a pioneer in children's well-being based on Heart Centered Learning work.

Dr. Mason worked to amplify her driving forces by increasing awareness and building evidence and credibility while reducing resisting forces by refuting her critics' arguments. Schools may find that some of these tactics, such as seeking funding for research, presenting at national conferences, and using social media to advertise use of the approach, are useful to them.

Implementing Visions Requires Change

Change is difficult for many. Some people may lose self-confidence and feel incompetent, needy, or powerless. Change requires effort and enthusiasm, and not everyone is naturally inclined to live with the excitement and challenges that accompany change. Implementing visions can involve a significant degree of transformation, which requires a leader to have purpose, resolve, and grit. It is essential for key stakeholders (staff, students, and families) to be involved in planning and executing change, to have opportunities to develop new skills required by the change, and to be able to turn to psychological support mechanisms put in place before, during, and after the change is implemented.

Consider Principal Melissa Usiak's journey as she describes how educators at her school went through a forming, storming, norming, and performing cycle when their population shifted and they needed to accommodate a significant number of students living in poverty.

Vision - Maintaining Collective Motivation and Enthusiasm

Dr. Melissa Usiak
Associate Professor Michigan State University
Former Principal

Our journey was just that, *our* journey. It is not to be thought of as *the* exemplar or *the* answer in creating a robust, collaborative school culture. There is no secret recipe, no silver bullet, or no magic to gain such gracious effort from my former colleagues for so many years. The foundation of all we accomplished was shaped by the relationships we worked to build and maintain—intentional, relentless relationship building from day one. The relationships grew under the guise of sharing evidence of need and coupling it with research. I made each decision transparently and built capacity with each and every staff member.

Leading Challenges

I was recently corresponding with one of my former second grade teachers. She ended the conversation with, "We would have done anything for you." And I think this is true. I applied positive pressure on our team time and again across seven years as their principal. They consistently met the challenges of change under my leadership, knowing our efforts would improve how we served our students and families. We began our journey by thoughtfully considering our stage of group development. Anytime leadership changed, the dynamics changed.

(Continued)

(Continued)

Here's what we did to successfully engage as a community:

- We started in a state of forming but moved through a storming phase as congenial collaboration faded, followed by norming and, finally, performing (see the explanations of these stages that follow).

- We spoke openly about these natural stages of teaming.

- We noticed that the significant changes in student demographics were causing great dissonance for the staff. They had never taught such a significant number of students living in poverty. Along with being a new team, this was reason for us to pause and have open dialogue about shared values, mission, and vision. We involved everyone in this process.

- We established that the process far outweighed any product of a neat and tidy list of values or well-displayed mission and vision statements. When we did this, we involved *everyone*. Many staff members, specifically paraeducators and recess supervisors, had never been engaged and invested in this type of work. This was the beginning of establishing collective ownership and building capacity across the entire school community. I truly feel that these initial exercises, investing in each and every person, shaped the remainder of our work during my tenure.

After we worked together to establish our values, mission, and vision, we were united in our efforts. We had developed relationships across roles, and we trusted and supported each other. Because we took the time to build a strong foundation, we were able to accomplish a lot. We were able to establish home visits, breakfast in the classroom, alternate recess, positive behavior intervention supports (PBIS), multitier support systems (MTSSs), goal-setting conferences, family literacy events, and authentic community-based partnerships and even moved to a balanced calendar. Each of these changes was driven by need and research and grounded in our mission, vision, and values.

Additionally, we practiced courage on a regular basis. At the end of my first year, I received a vase from my most veteran teacher with a small inscription on it, *Courage*. Yes, it took loads of courage to push against the norms of traditional schooling. We channeled this courage through those deliberate relationships that held each of us up and allowed us to embrace the next challenge. For all of these experiences, I am forever grateful. It was, by far, the best years of my career in K–12 public education.

To be successful, Principal Usiak focused on communication and relationships. She built relationships across all levels and involved everyone in the transition process. She sought out perspectives and gained people's trust and respect. She also encouraged self-awareness and openly discussed the team's current and future stages of development. Knowing how to recognize and handle each of the forming, storming, norming, and performing cycles of change is useful to any principal. Psychologist Bruce Tuckman (1965) developed this model to describe the stages teams typically experience as they evolve from a collection of strangers to a united group with common goals (MindTools Content Team, n.d.).

In the forming stage, the group is generally excited and polite. They're energized about the task, but there aren't clear roles and responsibilities yet. The group leader is instrumental in establishing clear objectives and helping the group get to know one another.

What objectives do you have for your team at this stage?

How will you help the group get to know one another better?

Principal Usiak reflects,

Anytime leadership changes, the dynamics changed. We started in a state of forming. There was excitement and new energy mixed with cautious optimism as we intentionally got to know one another and form relationships. After several months of creating trustful relationships, we felt comfortable speaking our minds and sharing opinions.

In the storming stage, the group may become more contentious. As roles are gradually defined and tasks are assigned, team members may push back or challenge each other. This is the stage in which many teams fail. Teams need a strong leader to mediate conflict, remind everyone of their shared goal, and clearly define expectations and workloads. The leader should remain positive, build trust and relationships, and ensure team members don't feel overwhelmed by unequal workloads or stressed by ill-defined responsibilities.

What is the shared goal you will remind everyone of when conflict arises?

How will you define expectations and workloads?

How can you build trust and a sense of community while remaining positive?

What systems will you use to guard against unequal workloads and ill-defined responsibilities?

Principal Usiak: "This would push us into the storming phase as congenial collaboration faded. This was not purgatory by any means but a natural space in which to find ourselves. It allowed us to be candid, transparent, and vulnerable."

In the norming stage, team members begin to resolve their differences, appreciate each other's strengths, and respect the leader's authority. Team members work through their conflict and get to know each other better. They feel more comfortable and are able to work together, communicate more honestly, and provide more constructive feedback. They are committed to the goal and make progress toward it. There is often overlap between storming and norming as new tasks and challenges come up. The leader must be aware of this and respond accordingly to keep the team working together and progressing. The leader should focus on team building and encouraging team members to take responsibility for advancing toward the goal.

How will you encourage your team to appreciate each other's strengths?

How will you create a space where team members feel safe expressing opinions that lead to healthy disagreements? How will you help team members resolve conflicts?

What norms will you put into place to ensure that the team regularly engages in constructive feedback?

Principal Usiak: "From vulnerability comes courage. We leveraged the opportunities to be honest about our shared values, common purpose, and collective ownership of the work and success of our school community."

Next is the performing stage. In this stage, everyone knows what's expected, and processes are in place. The leader can delegate most of his or her work and focus on supporting and developing the team members.

How will you check in with your team members to ensure everyone is doing the work agreed upon? Think back to the accountability you created in your action plan.

How will you develop your team, and what support can you provide to team members?

Principal Usiak: "It took a full year before we could truly experience performing, the final stage, where we could take action, evaluate effectiveness, and make necessary adjustments. We spoke openly about these natural stages of teaming."

You're Not Operating in a Vacuum

We have to remember that we're not executing our vision in a vacuum but in a complex system made up of interconnected parts. A school is composed of administrative and management personnel, teachers, students, parents, community members, and others. To make sense of this complexity, Peter Senge denoted five components to better understand our problem and get a better sense of where we are right now. His components are systems thinking, personal mastery, mental models, building shared vision, and team learning (Smith, 2001).

Systems thinking involves stepping back to think about and address the larger system. You must examine the interrelationships among the parts and consider downstream consequences and dependencies. Personal mastery involves continuously clarifying your vision and goals internally. You must focus your energy, develop patience, and see things objectively. We must also be aware and cognizant of mental models. These are deeply ingrained assumptions and patterns of thinking that are often subconscious. We need to reflect on these and how they may affect our thoughts and actions.

What are some personal assumptions and thought patterns that might bias this process?

What assumptions and thought patterns among staff might bias this process?

What assumptions and thought patterns among other stakeholders might bias this process?

Building a shared vision involves painting an inspiring and clear picture of what you seek to create. It needs to inspire commitment and excitement to guide and sustain everyone. Finally, there is team learning. This involves aligning and developing the team's capabilities. Working together and utilizing each member's strengths and capabilities will help you accomplish your goal.

Senge's framework provides guidance on how to successfully enact change in a complex setting. Some of the greatest challenges in the process of visioning are setting a collaborative goal, defining and initiating strategy, and sustaining the effort among your team members to meet the goal (see Chapter 6: Steps 5–8). We can recognize through this process that change is a constant and realize that a measure of successful change requires modifying basic human behavior. You need to inspire people and actually spur them to action.

The Art of Seeing Can Lead to Inspiration and Commitment

"Visioning helps people see that no matter where they are, their contributions are serving the purpose of the entire organization, not just in the areas that they directly work."

— *George Couros (2015)*

Building a shared vision begins by seeing clearly and creatively. It involves painting an inspiring and clear picture of what you see and seek to create. A vivid vision will go far to inspire the needed commitment and excitement to guide and sustain everyone. Finally, there is team learning. This involves aligning and developing the team's capabilities. Working together and utilizing each member's strengths and capabilities will help you accomplish your goal.

Good leaders must enlist the best efforts of trusted advisors within their organization to effectively define where *they are today* and where *they are going tomorrow*. Defining goals and then meeting them is accomplished by creating a sustained effort that is understood and implemented cooperatively. By recognizing the contributions that individuals, at all levels, bring to the good of an organization, we can consider introducing suggestions for improvement and sustained participation (Galbraith, 2018). Engagement, sustained effort, and improvement are hallmarks of achieving an established goal through visioning.

Committing to being laser-focused with a sustained commitment to an organization's goal is an unceasing challenge. Even when members of an organization or team are part of creating the vision, it can be difficult to maintain and sustain a commitment to the defined goals. We cannot state often enough the value of including all members of the team, leaders, and those who exhibit leadership qualities. All who have garnered respect among their peers should be charged with mentoring and nurturing the groups through the process of change. This involvement begins in the vision creation phase and must be sustained to the end for success.

Support From Advocacy Organizations

In addition to support from trusted advisors or consultants, school leaders may also find support for their vision from professional membership or advocacy organizations. In the area of STEM, for example, P21 is a prime example of an organization that was established to promote STEM exemplars. Each year, P21 highlights a cohort of schools and districts who are equipping their students with the necessary skills and knowledge for school, career, and life. They create case studies for each 21st century exemplar school or district to share their insights and stories to help guide others. In addition to these case studies, P21 holds an annual awards ceremony to celebrate each school or district's hard work, and they share insights, best practices, and updates via Twitter, to promote community, collaboration, and achievement so all students can experience the best of 21st century learning experiences (Battelle for Kids, 2016).

Teacher, principal, and superintendent membership organizations often provide forums for networking, advancing progressive ideas, stimulating educational improvements, and advocating for resources for support.

Advantages of joining an advocacy group include the following:

- Staying current on relevant research, policies, and legislation

- Opportunities to advocate for teachers, principals, and education

- A voice to convey needs and concerns to government agencies

- A forum for debate and discussion to move the conversation forward

- A sense of community and collaboration to keep you energized and motivated

- Gaining ideas and support for visioning

Visioning With Support From Member Organizations

Mark Terry, Deputy Director
Texas Elementary Principals and Supervisors Association

Mark Terry, a past president of the National Association of Elementary School Principals and current deputy director of the Texas Elementary Principals and Supervisors Association (TEPSA), explains the importance of visioning:

> During the more than 100 years that TEPSA has served our members, we have evolved as the needs of our principals and schools have changed. How does a school, or any organization for that matter, maintain relevance for its members over that amount of time? A commitment to a circular pattern of visioning could well be the answer.
>
> We consistently take a hard look at what is changing for our members, study how we should change to meet those needs, develop our strategies to meet those needs, evaluate the results, and start looking for the next change headed our way.
>
> How do you know where to look? Where's the next shift going to occur? Some changes are predictable: what do recent elections show us; what new technology is advancing, and how are our students and teachers using it; how is the economy doing; are there migration patterns to our state for which we have to account? For example, our state, Texas, has been growing at a rate of 70,000 students per year, and of those 70,000, most come from homes where English is not the language spoken. How does that affect the programs and services we offer our children?
>
> Another way that our organization helps students is by having a presence in the world of state and national politics. TEPSA must

continually assess how each generation of our members wants to participate. Do they want to merely be informed about how legislation is going to affect them? Do they want to be a part of a social media network that influences the actions of legislators? Our members are from several generations, each with its own unique ways of participating through our professional organization. If we are not visioning in a circular manner, we would quickly become irrelevant and cease to exist.

Connections to an Advocacy Group

Jennifer Mayes
MEMSPA State and Federal Relations Coordinator, 2014–2018
Principal, Luther C. Klager Elementary
Director, Manchester Early Childhood Center

When looking for support, it's important to seek the advice and help of those in your field. One way to do this is to join professional organizations for whatever aspect of education speaks to your needs. The value of membership in an organization can often be summed up in one word: relationships. However, the connections I have cultivated through MEMSPA extend beyond networking with colleagues and meeting other individuals in the profession. My personal experience has led to relationships with legislators at the state and federal levels.

Many of our elected officials have no experience in public education other than attending school themselves or through the lens of parenthood. But we all know that going to the doctor doesn't make us experts in the medical field any more than attending school makes us knowledgeable about the ins and outs of public education. If policy makers do not have trusted individuals with whom to confer regarding educational matters, who will they be listening to?

Advocacy does take time, but it is so worth it. When principals step away from the daily grind of their buildings to speak on behalf of students across the state and nation, it opens their eyes to new perspectives and elevates them to have an impact that extends beyond the walls of their own schools. Advocacy allows you to feel like you have helped shape legislation and are not just helpless individuals on the receiving end of mandates. And when you can advocate as an organization, the impact is astounding. Imagine 1,000 voices across the association uniting in a collective message to the men and women of Congress! Instead of a squeaky wheel, we become a roaring machine that cannot be unheard.

Sustainability

Although barriers arise that affect the initial implementation of visions, additional barriers can be expected over time. Most of us are familiar with even the best made plans going awry. Renee Owen, executive director of Rainbow Community School, discusses some of the barriers she faced as she guided her schools through change over a period of years.

Barriers to Becoming an Inclusive and Equitable Community

Renee Owen, Executive Director
Rainbow School
Asheville, North Carolina

Through our shared visioning process, Rainbow Community School agreed to become an inclusive and more equitable community. Like many progressive organizations, when Rainbow Community School decided to put *socially just* in our mission statement, we didn't fully understand the impact. After three years of massive change—including equity training for staff and parents, tripling the amount of financial aid available, declaring ourselves an *affirmative action school*, hiring an equity director, and much more—I didn't realize how much tension was bubbling underneath the surface. I learned the hard way that White people don't want to say out loud that seeing so many more Black and brown faces can make them uncomfortable and that paying higher tuition and other changes felt like too much of a sacrifice for some.

In the past, people would speak openly about any issues they had at our school, but this was different because people were afraid of being labeled *racist*. Of course, this also meant that Rainbow was not yet a truly inclusive place, and I was working hard to ensure it could be a safe space for people of color and people from marginalized economic situations.

As a leader, it was a situation in which I had to accept that I couldn't possibly make everyone happy. In the end, our leadership—both administrative and the board—had to stay true and committed to our stated values, even in the midst of some heavy personal sacrifice. We also had to bring the issue to the surface and talk about it, no matter how uncomfortable or ugly it was. Although there is always work to be done, we weathered this storm, and Rainbow Community School is now viewed as a leader and regional trainer in holistic equitable practices, but it was painful.

Missie also explains the challenges of maintaining an inspirational vision across the years:

> Our school is a living system. We change, we grow, and we improve all the time. By keeping our focus on our how we want our students to succeed, we cultivate new ideas, maintain applicability, and spark motivation across our school. Empowering collective voice of stakeholders ensures that our beliefs stay current and our passions stay relevant to those we serve.

One of the challenges of sustaining a vision through leadership is to ensure that the current culture in a school or district accepts change, new ideas, and ultimately grows stronger based on the variations. As a school principal, Missie celebrated retirements, added special education programs, welcomed new administrators, and hired a variety of staff with diverse strengths. The staff that she hired sixteen years ago are the same human beings, yet they have grown in both their careers as well as in their personal experiences. "The collective vision that our school held dear ten years ago is similar to our current vision, but it's not the same. It's owned and accentuated by those teaching, supporting, and leading our school today."

She intentionally takes time as a staff to revisit what's valued, where they see their efforts headed, and all that motivates them toward this success. They focus on teamwork and connections. Most importantly, they listen to each other. By truly hearing our colleagues, our opinions and ideas become shared. At staff meetings, department gatherings, and grade-level discussions questions such as "Where are we?" or "Where do we need to be?" or "What do we need to get there?" are discussed. In addition, the team listens to concerns and barriers and brainstorms solutions. This process empowers everyone involved to press forward.

Missie elaborates:

> *The majority of educators are talented individuals that want to do what's right for kids. Yet, not everyone agrees on the best path to get to the same end. In my school, we value our positive culture, we prioritize acknowledgment of all human beings, and we collectively work to minimize negative dynamics such as gossip. We believe that the impact of a*

supportive climate throughout the school makes our work impactful, inspirational, and meaningful as a school and a workplace.

As new staff join her school, she refocuses on their beliefs and reiterates their cultural expectations: (1) we acknowledge each other; (2) we work to have trusted work friends that will listen to our concerns and keep our venting private; (3) we operate with intentional gratitude; and (4) we share and celebrate personal joys and successes. With these elements at the core belief system of their visioning work, they have been able to openly trust and explore their differences. Most importantly, they have learned to find common ground and build their team from there up. Their collective vision is their priority, as it ensures sustainability of the essential beliefs.

Focus, Priorities, and Goal Setting

Too often teams can't identify their most important goals, don't know what they should be focusing on, don't know how to measure success, and don't keep track of their progress. In their book, *The 4 Disciplines of Execution*, Chris McChesney, Sean Covey, and Jim Huling (2012) outline four principles organizations should embrace to achieve their goals and realize their vision.

Discipline One: Focus on the Wildly Important. Not everything can be at the top of our list of priorities. To be clear about the importance of a vision and strategies for implementation, highlight a few essential points to assure that the focus is maintained. Focus on less, so you can achieve more.

What are the three points at the top of your list?

Discipline Two: Act on Lead Measures. "While a lag measure tells you if you've achieved the goal, a lead measure tells you if you are likely to achieve the goal" (McChesney et al., 2012). Instead of tracking lag measures that don't allow for real-time optimization, the authors identify lead measures that predict success. Once you identify and track activities, you will be more in control of accomplishing your important goals.

What are potential lead measures?

Lagging and Lead Measures at MEMSPA

In 2014, MEMSPA, a community of principals dedicated to advocating, leading, and learning, established lagging measures focused on increased membership, financial stability with increased fund equity, growth in professional development opportunities, and member participation.

MEMSPA's lead measures included doubling professional development opportunities for members, increasing member engagement via social media such as Facebook and LinkedIn, and developing a weekly Twitter chat, increasing advocacy with a third-party advocacy group that brought two additional lobbyists for the association.

By Year Five, fund equity grew to 100 percent, membership was up 10 percent, and membership participation in MEMSPA's professional development increased by 20 percent.

Discipline Three: Keep a Compelling Scoreboard. Keeping score affects how people and teams play the game. Employees are emotionally engaged and committed to the goals and vision of the organization when they score.

In MEMSPA, staff and the board of directors review membership growth and financial statements on a quarterly basis to track progress and see how they're doing. The most effective scoreboard is one employees know about and help design.

What are some ideas for scoreboards that might work for your school or district?

Discipline Four: Create a Cadence of Accountability. It requires frequent check-ins and allows team members to share their progress and hold each other accountable for producing significant results. When the members of an organization can identify measured improvement and incremental success, they're motivated even more to reach the finish line.

In their book, Chris McChesney and colleagues (2012) describe the essential role that accountability plays in sustaining a vision: "81% of people surveyed said they were not held accountable for regular progress on the organization's goals and the goals were not translated into specific actions" (p. 5–6). According to their research, people who aren't sure what the goal is aren't committed to it. People may not know the specifics of what is expected of them. There may also be a lack of follow-through in holding them accountable to the goals of the vision. Furthermore, when all members in an organization observe leaders living and practicing strategies that lead to goal success, they will be more likely to follow. They also will be more willing to participate with enthusiasm and high levels of motivation if the desired outcomes are realistic and attainable.

MEMSPA staff and leadership held stakeholders accountable with frequent check-ins, goal progress updates, and celebrations of small successes every quarterly meeting.

How often will you have check-ins?

How will your team hold each other accountable to reaching your goals?

When Leadership Changes

One of the most challenging aspects to sustain a vision is how to maintain it when a leader moves on. It is one thing to experience the sense of community and commitment to change with an enthusiastic proponent at the helm. It is something else for a vision to survive a change of leadership. One way to safeguard a vision is to make sure that the ownership is diffused across the organization.

Collaborative Visioning Creates Sustainable Change

Allyson Apsey, Principal
Quincy Elementary School
Zeeland, Michigan

When a leader develops a vision for an organization and then goes about the business of making it happen, successful change can take hold. However, when that leader moves on to a new job, that vision often goes away with him or her. Sustainable change cannot be reliant upon only one person. Culture doesn't change through the will of a leader alone. *Buy-in* is a term that implies that leadership is an act of salesmanship, but leadership is not about selling a vision. It is about collaboratively creating a vision. A visionary leader who can create sustainable change and turn around an organization's culture knows the importance of communication, meeting people where they are, and empowering individuals to take part in not only the steps to make a vision a reality but in the creation of the vision itself.

Educational leaders Shelley Burgess and Beth Houf (2017) wrote about this idea in their book *Lead Like a Pirate*. They said, "People are less likely to tear down systems they help to build" (p. 23). When people in an organization are invested at a grassroots level, they will work their tails off to make a vision a reality.

Conclusions—Leveraging Communities Near and Far to Overcome Barriers to Sustainability

In this chapter, we showed you how beneficial it is to work not just with your school or district community but also the larger community that exists in professional organizations like principals' associations or education advocacy organizations. Mark Terry, deputy director of TEPSA, shared how he grew this organization by leveraging past professional connections he made in other organizations. Jennifer Mayes, MEMSPA state and federal relations coordinator, shared how her involvement in professional organizations connected her to politicians who needed to hear her experiences to make informed policy decisions. We also discussed how to sustain a vision even after the leader who conceived it moves on by inspiring other school and district leaders to become integral members of the visioning process.

Practical Points to Ponder

- Why do we ask you to consider the art of seeing? What talents and skills do artists bring to their canvasses, and why might visioning be compared to the creative process of an artist?

- What are some of the reasons that faculty and staff might have a negative reaction to visioning?

(Continued)

(Continued)

- Do you have any ideas for helping others set aside any prior negative experiences with visioning?

   In this time of relative silence on the national educational front, local leaders have the opportunity to step into the leadership void that is apparent. It is a time when leaders can ask questions about deep learning, questions such as the ones Michael Fullan and colleagues (2018) pose regarding learning: where is learning happening, and how should we approach measuring success? How do these questions affect the visions you are already contemplating, even as you realize the value of moving forward at the right time and pace with sufficient support and encouragement from others you trust?

Your Path to Sustainability

Whether it be "meeting in circles" (i.e., Renee Owen and the Rainbow Community School), turning to advocacy groups for support, finding additional resources, or increasing opportunities for celebrations of success, there are a multitude of strategies that will enhance the likelihood that your vision will result in long-term and lasting change.

Ideas for Leading and Learning

- An effective vision allows us to see what's ahead and where we need to travel as an organization. For your school family, what are the three core beliefs held about students, learning, and the school community?

- Consider visioning from the perspective of another leader or staff member in your school. What would you expect them to agree on in your framework of vision, and what would you anticipate them disagreeing with?

- In our approach to visioning, we suggest considering voices and input that travel in our pipeline to create a strong outcome. Who among your school stakeholders influences the direction you head? Whose voice needs to be elevated to a higher level? Who needs to listen?

Resources to Explore

Scan the QR Code or visit https://resources.corwin.com/visioningonward to access live links to this book's online resources.

PART III

VISIONING AT THE MACRO LEVEL

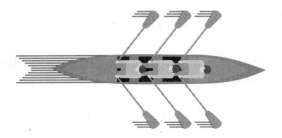

Chapter 8

FUTURE VISIONING—HERE AND ACROSS THE GLOBE

Where there is no vision, the people perish.

—Proverbs 29:18

Asuccessful vision relies on current and commonly understood definitions and measures of student success. It should also reflect the full range of what learners must know and be able to do to be successful inside and outside of the classroom.

In *Visioning Onward*, we have focused on the future of education, considering particularly how school leaders can engage their local schools in visioning for their futures. As you prepare for your visioning journey with staff, it may be helpful to consider not only the power of visioning but also the budding innovations that may have an impact on tomorrow. Although technological advances might be forces that are most quickly driving change in our society, we must take into consideration all of the ways that the changing landscape of our culture affect education. What follow are some educational trends that are currently having an impact on how schools operate. Once you take these trends into account, you'll want to adjust your vision accordingly.

Trends in Education Affecting How Schools Operate

- STEM/STEAM and technology

- Social media

- Preparing students for careers in an uncertain future

- Increasing student diversity

- Toxic levels of stress on staff and students

- New understandings of neuroscience regarding how students learn

- Social emotional learning

Aaron Brengard provides a good example of a principal who considered many of these points in working with his staff on developing and implementing visions at both Katherine Smith Elementary and also Bulldog Tech (see Chapters 1 and 2).

The vision statement of Frost Elementary Schools in Allegany School District in Maryland also reflects these values:

The vision at Frost Elementary School is to prepare and motivate our students for a rapidly changing world by instilling in them critical thinking skills, a global perspective, and a respect for core values of honesty, loyalty, perseverance, and compassion. Students will have success for today and be prepared for tomorrow.

(Allegany County Public Schools, 2019)

Change and Its Drivers

What is catalyst for change? Usually we find that there are underlying sources of tension or friction as those with a vision seek ways to develop support for their visions. Whether it be an innovative technology, a new way of addressing needs or activities, or other ways to enhance our work and our lives, there are specific factors that help *escalate* or *drive* change. These drivers help create a sense of urgency and overcome the complacency that is often a stumbling block to change. In this chapter, we will discuss six change drivers that are significantly altering the landscape of education as we have known it. By keeping these change drivers at the forefront of your thinking, you and your leadership team will be better prepared to draft vision and mission statements that will better serve your students.

Change Drivers

1. Automating choices
2. Civic superpowers
3. Accelerating brains
4. Toxic narratives
5. Remaking geographies
6. Social emotional and Heart Centered Learning

Technology and Our Way of Being and Doing

Perhaps the educational trend that is most obvious right now is the expansion of our digital world. eSchool News is a leading provider of news and information to help K–12 decision makers successfully use technology and the internet. In a recent eSchool News article, Christine Feher (2019) describes ten trends affecting K–12 education, including increased use of the following:

- Immersive technologies, including augmented and virtual reality

- Assistive technologies and integrated learning to update published information and assist students as they pursue knowledge at a greater depth

- Digital backpacks that will include information on students' learning, academic performance, and notes from previous educators—these will follow individual students across grade levels and will make it easier to personalize learning

- More personalized learning to allow students to pursue their own goals and better monitoring of individualized progress

- Stronger cybersecurity to begin to address privacy concerns about student data

As these are implemented, Feher envisions a greater interface between edtech companies and schools. The need for a growing interface can be seen by echoes of needs and concerns for matching school capabilities with a proliferation of high-tech devices.

In such a rapidly changing world, nonprofits have formed to help educators stay abreast of emerging trends. For example, Knowledge-Works partners with K–12 educators, policy makers, and education stakeholders to help them innovate and prepare for the future by forecasting trends to vision a way forward. Katherine Prince, vice president of Strategic Insight, explains, "KnowledgeWorks publishes a new forecast every 3 years based on a 10-year time horizon when looking into the future . . . to provide education stakeholders with a rigorous view of the external environment to better inform their strategic planning and visioning work" (KnowledgeWorks, 2018).

KnowledgeWorks's (2018) most recent forecast, *Forecast 5.0—The Future of Learning: Navigating the Future of Learning*, can serve as your sextant in guiding your visioning process and the subsequent implementation. It can give you a clearer picture of the kaleidoscope of ever-changing landscapes and societal forces having an impact on your schools, district, and community. The goal is to help education decision makers think through implications, both positive and negative, and make sense of what's on the horizon within their specific context. *Forecast 5.0* helps leaders gauge how their vision of the here-and-now matches up against what will be. They have identified five drivers of change (to which we've added a sixth—social emotional and Heart Centered Learning): automating choices, civic superpowers, accelerating brains, toxic narratives, and remaking geographies. Artificial intelligence (AI) and algorithms are increasingly automating our choices, engaged citizens and organizations are seeking to rebalance power, easily accessible tools and insights are reshaping and extending our thinking, outdated systems and success metrics are contributing to increased stress and mental health issues, and communities are trying to unite and remake themselves in the face of deep transitions.

Unwanted Side Effects of Too Much Technology

One concern educators and many others have had for quite a while is that with the rising use of technology, face-to-face communication has been reduced. Many opt for texting over placing a phone call, and many youth enjoy virtual games rather than getting together for in-person activities. The Pew Research Center reported that in 2019, "70% of Americans were using social media to connect with one another, engage with news content, share information, and entertain themselves."

A 2019 follow-up study detailed the resulting toll on student emotional well-being due to social media (Menasce & Graf, 2019):

- 71 percent of students thought anxiety and depression are major problems for their peers.

- 61 percent felt pressure to get good grades.

- 54 to 55 percent indicated alcohol and drug use and bullying were major concerns.

- 28 to 29 percent felt pressure to fit in and look good.

According to the National Survey of Children's Health, anxiety diagnoses in students ages six to seventeen spiked 20 percent between 2007 and 2012 (Nutt, 2018). This spike in anxiety is shown in Figure 8.1.

When we consider schools of the future with large digital components, we must also find ways to address the collateral stress and trauma that people are facing all over the world. As you complete the visioning process, attempt to balance the use of technology with in-person human interaction. Using technology collaboratively can help ensure that technology becomes a tool to enhance rather than replace one-on-one discourse.

Figure 8.1   Student Anxiety on the Rise

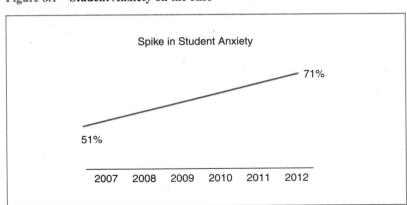

Change Driver 1—Automating Choices

Much has been made of algorithms and AI, which have become increasingly ubiquitous—for good reason. With the rise of Amazon Dash providing one-touch, shopping convenience, Google Home adjusting the lights in our living rooms, Siri providing up-to-the-minute reports on sports scores and the weather, and Netflix recommending our next movie, we have ready examples of how AI is becoming increasingly embedded in our daily lives.

Futurist Daniel Burrus (2017), author of *The Anticipatory Organization*, concurs. He helps organizations identify the top technology-driven trends that will shape our collective future. Here is part of his list for K–12 education:

1. Virtualizing data storage, desktops, software applications, and broadband networking
2. Smart, voice-enabled devices and virtual e-assistants
3. Increasing intelligence of the internet of things (IoT)
4. Smarter smartphones and tablets and increasingly smarter mobile apps that automate process innovation

Teachers and principals are likely to find that these one-touch devices will be a central part of our teaching environment in the near future. Just as these devices help answer trivia questions such as "Who won the Super Bowl in 1975?", they may become more available to classrooms with a "Siri center" for an assignment to find facts. Or they may propel classroom Jeopardy to a whole new level as teams scramble to answer increasingly complex questions with an electronic assistant. Coupled with creativity, the possibilities are endless. Teachers could also set up classrooms for a scavenger hunt for teams with opportunities to find facts, have a virtual experience, drop in on a video, and record results on a holograph. There may even be content-specific mini-devices that function as calculators. Consider, for example, a "STEM-assist" that guides you through questions to problem solve and/or provide a way to record results for trials when experimenting and implementing student designs.

Electronic Assistants

Amazon is one company investing heavily in preparing students and teachers for the reality of an autonomous future. Amazon automation will affect schools' information technology "back office" in many ways. Take, for example, the Amazon Dash button. These physical key fobs can be programmed to reorder a range of household supplies from Amazon with a click of the Dash button. The ingenious IoT technology behind Dash is a cloud-based programming platform that leverages Wi-Fi to link the customizable key fobs with your account at Amazon.com.

Could it be that these electronic assistants could help schools become safer environments with not only automated door locks but also instantaneous tracking of anyone who enters a building? Combined with thumbprint identification process, could it be that the system could alert staff to suspicious activity within a matter of seconds? Amazon already provides opportunities to teach students how to program Dash buttons in the classroom with a full set of curricular resources. Known as the Amazon Web Services (AWS) IoT Button, students can

> code the button's logic in the cloud to configure button clicks to count or track items, call or alert someone, start or stop something, order services, or even provide feedback. For example, you can click the button to unlock or start a car, open your garage door, call a cab, call your spouse or a customer service representative, track the use of common household chores, medications, or products, or remotely control your home appliances.
>
> (Amazon Web Services, 2019)

While increasing digitalization and an expanded IoT have some appeal, they come with a warning about our loss of individual privacy and control over our personal data. As futurist Daniel Burrus describes, we must be alert to the possibly of the ever watchful Big Brother, loss of privacy, or data misuse for less than altruistic reasons.

Key Learning 8.1

Automating Choices—Considerations for Classrooms

Review Change Driver 1. Consider how automating choices can have an impact on your school or district. It may even affect your vision for your school and district's future. How might automatization change the gadgets available in your classrooms? What will be the impact on things such as your learning centers, approaches to collaborative learning, or student assignments?

Change Driver 2—Civic Superpowers

The rise of automation has created great income disparities between rich and poor countries as well as the haves and have-nots within countries like the United States. The current public displeasure with our government institutions to effectively address economic inequality has added pressure on the public education system to provide multiple pathways to prosperity for the next generation of citizens. Fortunately, thousands of not-for-profit institutions, volunteer organizations, and individual philanthropists are flexing their civic muscles to support school leaders in these efforts. Many of these initiatives are achieving impact at a scale like never before by harnessing the same disruptive technologies that have created the inequalities.

There is no better example than Bill and Melinda Gates, who have pledged to give away their estimated $100 billion fortune earned by automating the white-collar workforce with Microsoft Windows, Office, and Cloud. Since 2009, their foundation has created $1.45 billion in a variety of innovative education initiatives (Piper, 2019). For example, the Big History Project (BHP), is a free, open, and online "supercharged social studies curriculum" for middle and high school students that comes complete with in-person and online professional development and other free out-of-the-box tools to help free up teaching time to refocus on individual student instruction (Big History Project, n.d.).

More than 1,600 teachers and 80,000 students worldwide have participated in BHP, which aims to provide all students with access to such "big thinking" history teaching. The Gates Foundation created, curated, tested, and continually improved BHP resources to help teachers teach big, cosmic, and global history (Bain, 2015).

Consider also the Giving Pledge, started by the Gateses and Warren Buffett in 2010. They were joined by forty of the wealthiest families around the globe in making a commitment to give away more than half of their amassed wealth to eleven important causes, with education chief among them (Clifford, 2017). To date, the initiative has received 190 pledgers from thirty states and twenty-two countries. See the full list of pledge signatories at **Online Resource 8.1**.

What are the implications for our educational future? Although philanthropies support many worthwhile causes, there is some danger that the super wealthy could in essence dictate curricula and influence who has access to the new knowledge assets that are made available through their private funding.

Change Driver 3—Accelerating Brains

The rapid advance in information technology this century is matched by advances in neuroscience research. Increasingly, these are combining to transform our cognitive abilities in both intended and unintended ways. This raises incredible ethical questions and generates sensational headlines that seem torn from the pages of science-fiction novels yet are on the front page of the *New York Times*. The latest neurotechnology is bent on enhancing human cognition by promising to erase brain-based challenges to learning. Whether it's capable of that though is up for debate.

A controversy involving Neurocore landed on the front page of the *New York Times* political section in 2018 because the company lost an appeal before the National Advertising Review Board (Green, 2018). Neurocore's claims of curbing and curing attention deficit disorder, depression, and autism without medication were deemed misleading due to mixed research findings and unscientific internal studies. US Education Secretary Betsy DeVos's investment, valued at $5 million to $25 million, in the "brain-performance" technology startup propelled the story to the headlines.

Halo Neuroscience develops and markets neurotechnology that help individuals "unlock their true potential." Their first product, Halo Sport 2, is an all-in-one, over-the-ear headset that helps accelerate skill and strength acquisition. Halo uses electrical currents to stimulate the part

(Continued)

(Continued)

of the brain that controls motion—the motor cortex. This is the area that helped you learn to ride a bike and that stores your "muscle memories." The ability to learn these new skills is called *neuroplasticity*. The electric pulses from the Halo Sport 2 headset supercharge your brain's natural plasticity and help you learn movements faster. As the podcast summed it up, "It seems we're engineering faster learning brains. Just imagine what can happen—all the risks and all the gains" (Fake, 2019).

According to the latest research published in the peer-reviewed journal, *Frontiers in Society*, the Halo Sport 2 "enhances cycling (bicycling) performance by 17 percent" in terms of improved mean power output and cognitive performance (Huang, Deng, Zheng, & Liu, 2019). In their research-Huang and colleagues measured cognition functions with a test of executive functioning that measures things such as information processing speed, sustaining attention, interference, and inhibition (see also Chang, Chu, Wang, Song, and Wei, 2015). The implications of this research for academic performance are not clear at this time.

Figure 8.2   Halo Sport 2's Effect on Skill and Strength Acquisition

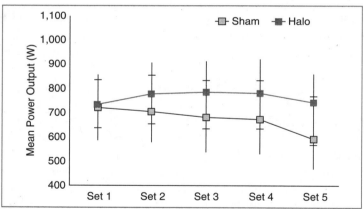

If these evidence-based claims hold up, don't be surprised to see some of your high school athletes sporting these during conditioning drills. (It should be noted that Halo Neuroscience does not recommend use by students less than eighteen years of age.)

Should This Exist?, a podcast hosted by Caterina Fake, is an excellent resource for future-proofing your visioning. During an interview with Fake, Dr. Daniel Chao, CEO and cofounder of Halo said,

"We know the brain is an electrical organ and we've known this for literally hundreds of years. . . . What if we used electricity to retune the brain circuits—potentially to treat disease, potentially to extract more performance out of otherwise healthy people?" (Fake, 2019).

Neuroplasticity and Equity

Addressing the equity issue, *Should This Exist?* host Caterina Fake (2019) puts a positive spin on Halo Sport 2 by assuming the product would be used "presumably when you're learning in school or [by] people who have just not had the same advantages as others [so they] could catch up more quickly." Chao responded with equal optimism:

> I think what our product does is it makes your brain temporarily kid-like. It makes it so that it's spongier, and it can absorb information, for a window of time of course, not permanently. But you could take advantage of this window of time to kind of shove more information in and have it stick to a greater extent. So yeah, if someone grew up in an environment where they didn't have all the privileges of the learning opportunities, and the best teachers, and the best life experiences, and into adulthood they were afforded these opportunities, there's an opportunity to use a technology like this to play catch up.

(Fake, 2019)

Mindfulness and Executive Functioning

In addition to sci-fi-esque brain technology, there are also ways to improve and extend our thinking without technology. Mindfulness has enjoyed widespread popularity recently, and research studies have demonstrated positive impacts of mindfulness on executive functioning (EF), a core set of cognitive functions responsible for planning, organizing, and self-regulating.

In a study of 191 third graders, a prerecorded mindfulness-based social emotional learning program significantly improved reading and science grades as well as classroom behavior (Bakosh, Snow, Tobias, Houlihan, & Barbosa-Leiker, 2016). The authors speculate that an improvement in EF skills led to an increased ability to pay attention and improved grades. Flook et al. (2010) found that students who most needed EF skills benefited the most from mindfulness-based interventions. EF is a critical component of self-regulation that develops rapidly across childhood, contributing to cognitive flexibility, working memory, and inhibitory control (Zelazo et al., 2008). EF skills provide the foundation for learning; they are linked to school readiness, successful participation in classroom learning (e.g., persistence, self-reliance, and motivation), and school success across a range of outcomes (Blair, Zelazo, & Greenberg 2016; Clark, Pritchard, & Woodward, 2010).

Change Driver 4—Toxic Narratives

Society today seems to be at an inflection point in terms of the narratives and metrics used to define individual success and their impact on student achievement. Thanks in part to the rise of social media and the 24/7 hype cycle, other people's aspirations, choices, and behaviors are becoming increasingly detrimental to individual and societal health, which in turn, are contributing to growing toxicity in governmental institutions and public education systems. The combined impact of many events throughout the world and the rapidity of information and knowledge dissemination is such that we are bombarded with negativity, fears, and concerns, raising levels of anxiety for many today. This section will cover stress and its impact not only on students but also on things such as career choices, the shortage of teachers, and the implications for the future of education.

Without question, the US public education system's narrative has been focused exclusively on college attainment as an indicator of school system success during the No Child Left Behind era.

- More than 35 states have replaced state graduation tests with college entrance exams such as the ACT and SAT.

- The added emphasis on going to college has increased the percentage of students—61 percent—indicating future plans to attend a four-year college who feel pressure to earn good grades. That percentage increases to 70 percent when stressing over acceptance by the college of their choice.

Stress

When we consider visioning for the future of schools, it will be helpful to also examine the factors that are affecting students' mindsets today and in the near future. Students today are under more academic pressure than ever to succeed, thereby increasing the amount of stress children feel in the classroom. Not only are students subject to stress related to school performance, but they are also subject to a multitude of other stress factors including peer pressure, bullying, parental divorce, illness, neglect, abuse, violence, injustice, death or loss, and discrimination. All of these additional stressors make it extremely hard for students to focus on learning, and they are exceptionally harmful to students' long-term health and well-being (Thoits, 2010).

When children do not have healthy ways of coping with these stressors, this can also lead to behavioral problems in school such as hostility toward the teacher and other students, disregard for school rules, and inattention during learning.

Not surprisingly, teachers describe student behavioral problems as one of the primary sources of their own stress, with standardized testing and unstable school leadership as other major sources (Greenberg, Brown, & Abenavoli, 2016). Teacher exhaustion and burnout result in a lack of effective teaching and a lack of compassion and empathy for students, thereby leading to a vicious cycle of student–teacher stress in the school environment. Specifically, the results of the Arens and Morin (2016) study demonstrated direct negative correlations between teachers' emotional exhaustion and the class average of students' school grades, standardized achievement test scores, school satisfaction, and perceptions of teacher support.

The Future of Employment

The anxiety over near-term career success portends looming concern over what jobs will be awaiting high school graduates. Martin Ford (2015), futurist and author of *Rise of the Robots: Technology and the Threat of a Jobless Future*, explains the jobs that are most at risk are those that "are on some level routine, repetitive, and predictable."

In the 2019 Global Human Capital trends report, international consulting firm Deloitte (2019) provides a guide for organizations seeking to navigate the changing employment landscape. The report indicates the following:

- Alternative workforces of contracted employees will increasingly fill the ranks of global corporations.

- This will place even more emphasis on 21st century collaboration, communication, and leadership skills.

- It will also require the transformation of employment experience to human experience by putting meaning back into work.

- Emphasis will shift to organizational performance over individual achievement as work becomes more of a team sport.

- The resulting economic awards will focus more on closing the equity pay gap.

- Professional learning will become lifelong and part of the flow of life.

A clear trend related to toxic narratives that threatens school visions is the cataclysmic decline of K–12 teaching as a career choice. A 2019 report by the Economic Policy Institute (EPI) indicates that high-poverty schools will suffer the most from the shortage of credentialed teachers (Garcia & Weiss, 2019). The report cites high certification requirements versus low pay as significant factors in high school graduates' decisions not to enter the profession and newly minted teachers' choices to leave. The EPI study found "roughly 60% of US teachers took on additional work during the school year to supplement poor compensation." A teacher shortage affects visioning for the future of education in several ways: (1) the "tide of change" may need to be adjusted either to address the impact of the shortage or to insert ideas to reverse the decline; (2) as we educate students and help them consider potential careers, will society benefit from a greater focus on their role furthering best practices in education, including best practices to encourage people to entertain the possibility of careers as teachers; and (3) what is the combined significance of an increase in technology and automatization and a decline in the number of teachers?

These contemporary economic considerations will continue to most significantly influence the changing geography—so much so that the Foresight team at KnowledgeWorks expanded the time horizon for their 2017 study *The Future of Learning: Redefining Readiness From the Inside Out* (Prince, 2017). Although this work focused more on the impact of technology rather than the impending teacher shortage, the issues are interrelated. "By taking our perspective out to 2040," Katherine Prince explains, "the trends impacting the future of work become very stark and provides a more expansive view for preparing students in the 21st Century." This trend provides an opportunity to explore both how to gain the greatest benefits from teacher–pupil face-to-face interactions and also how evolving enhanced technologies can assist with instructional delivery.

Teacher Shortages in Michigan

According to a recent report from Michigan (Citizens Research Council of Michigan, 2019), enrollment in Michigan teacher-prep programs has declined 66 percent over a recent seven-year period. Highly qualified teachers are key to any school's visioning success. That is why, more and more, school leaders are changing the narrative (i.e., increasing the number of teachers) by turning to alternative routes to teacher licensing and certification. Just this year, Kent Intermediate School District (ISD) in Grand Rapids, Michigan, launched its Teacher Cadet Program, focusing on preparing career and technical education (CTE) teachers for its countywide CTE programming. The Kent ISD Teacher Cadet program builds on the success of the local district teacher academies that seek to address the broader issue. Grand Rapids Public Schools, the largest district in Kent County, also announced the launch of its new Academy of Teaching and Learning in the fall of 2019, with the goal of recruiting up to ninety high school graduates to participate in the "fast track" to college graduation and a waiting teaching career.

Change Driver 5—Remaking Geographies

Another major driver in our collective future (i.e., not only as a driver for your local school or district but as a driver affecting the future of education) is the reshaping of local geographies in response to economic transition and climate, political, and social volatility. Katherine Prince (2019) of KnowledgeWorks indicated three global influencers that are remaking geographies:

- Contemporary economic considerations
- Climate-based disruption
- Global immigration patterns

Regardless of the national politics surrounding immigration, it is hard to deny the 2019 humanitarian crisis at the United States–Mexico border. The political and economic upheaval and unrest in Latin American has caused more than 100,000 refugees to flee north and seek asylum in the United States. More than 1 million immigrants attempted entrance in the twelve-month period ending in April 2019 (Rigaud et al., 2018). Immigration courts are overloaded with 800,000 pending cases, and these numbers are expected to climb given the economic and civil unrest in El Salvador (crime), Honduras (climate), Brazil (economics), and Venezuela (politics).

As it relates to climate change disaffecting Honduran emigres, Kirk Semple (2019) from *The New York Times* reported a surge in climate change-related cases from that Central American country, citing,

> Gradually rising temperatures, more extreme weather events, and increasingly unpredictable patterns—like rain not falling when it should, or pouring when it shouldn't—have disrupted growing cycles and promoted the relentless spread of pests.

> The obstacles have cut crop production or wiped out entire harvests, leaving already poor families destitute . . . [and] the livelihoods of millions of people at stake…The outlook for the region seems bleak (April 2019).

That's 2.6 million low-skill, low-wage workers disrupted by climate out of a Honduran population of 9.3 million, which is surrounded by other countries with agricultural-based economies. With the world only getting warmer, the ranks of Central American immigrants could swell to more than 5 million in the coming decade (Webber, 2018).

Migration patterns within the United States are also shifting, partly because of changing weather patterns and an aging population. A *Business Insider* article by Andy Kiersz (2019) sums it up with this headline "A Lot of Americans Are Moving South—and Many Are Heading to Florida."

This migration has significant ramifications for state agencies and local school districts because economic vitality also leaves with the people, especially when the people leaving are affluent. According to CBS News, "America's wealthy households are increasingly moving to coastal cities on both sides of the country, but those with more modest incomes are either relocating to or being pushed into the nation's Rust Belt" (Leefeldt, 2018; Romem, 2018).

Although this shifting geography has contributed to income and job opportunity inequality, it has also led to increased racial and socioeconomic diversity in schools across the nation. The US Department of Education (DOE) recognizes that when schools are aware of and celebrate diversity, students will be more prepared to work with people from different cultures in our 21st century workforce. The DOE (2017) published *Improving Outcomes for All Students: Strategies and Considerations to Increase Student Diversity*, which provides schools with a framework to ensure that they are keeping pace with the increased diversity of our nation. To help schools with this task, the DOE has created several grant programs that award funding to schools with diverse populations to provide a more equitable education for all students. These programs include the following:

- **Online Resource 8.2** Investing in Innovation

- **Online Resource 8.3** Opening Doors, Expanding Opportunities

- **Online Resource 8.4** Magnet Schools Assistance Program

- **Online Resource 8.5** Charter Schools Program

- **Online Resource 8.6** School Improvement Grants Program

- **Online Resource 8.7** Promise Neighborhoods

We invite you to access the live links to these programs from the book's web page to learn more about them.

Celebrating diversity also builds community. We can all learn from cultures different from our own. When you look at the diversity of your student population, consider how these demographics align with the diversity of your staff population. Do your students have examples of adults who look like them and come from the same socioeconomic background as them? If not, can diversity be one criterion you consider when hiring new employees, especially school-based mental health workers?

When we think about how to respond to the ways diversity affects our district or school building systems, it can be helpful to look outside our cities, states, and country to examples of work being done around the globe. Thankfully, many scholars have devoted their lives to compiling best practices from countries whose educational systems produce students who are academically, socially, and emotionally well.

Change Driver 6—Social Emotional and Heart Centered Learning

Social emotional learning is currently a hot topic among school leaders internationally and domestically (DePaoli, Atwell, & Bridgeland, 2017). For decades, a growing body of research has documented the positive effects of social emotional learning on individuals and communities (Durlak, Weissberg, Dymnicki, Taylor, & Schellinger, 2011; O'Connor, Blewitt, Nolan, & Skouteris, 2018). Now school leaders are implementing these programs to various levels of rigor and success (DePaoli et al., 2017). School leaders interested in visioning should be aware of a few trends in social emotional learning.

- When social emotional learning is implemented well, it involves many different stakeholders from the district, community, and classroom levels (CASEL, 2018).

- Many states are articulating social emotional learning competencies in their educational policy based upon five key competencies that the research agrees upon. All fifty states have done so for elementary school, and the Collaborative for Academic, Social, and Emotional Learning (CASEL) projects them to follow suit through the twelfth grade (Dusenbury, Weissberg, Goren, & Domitrovich, 2014).

- There is a dearth of social emotional learning assessments that are practical, cost-effective, and scalable (Berg et al., 2017; McKown, 2015).

- Students want social emotional learning programs as much as principals do. Fewer than half of high schoolers nationally surveyed believed that their schools did a good job of helping them develop key social emotional learning skills (DePaoli et al, 2017).

Many education visioning pioneers understand that to develop a student, we cannot forget to nurture not only their thinking but also their ability to interact with others. The 21st century workforce requires students to be excellent collaborators. Just as we must give students the tools and strategies to read, write, and complete math problems, social skills must be taught. Brené Brown, a research professor at University of Houston and former social worker, urges teachers to look at students holistically and ask themselves, "How can I show this child that I love them so they feel safe to learn?" She hopes that teachers will resist the instinct to label any student a "problem child" and instead ask themselves what difficulties in that student's life may have led to his or her disruptive behaviors, and how can I help him or her learn more effective coping mechanisms? She reminds us: "Connection is why we're here; it is what gives purpose and meaning to our lives" (Brown, 2015).

Heart Centered Learning

Although children's well-being will be furthered with a holistic approach that is inclusive of social emotional learning, the prevalence of trauma suggests that children's well-being will rest with more than teaching children social skills or framing learning with references to character education. In addition to stress, students are increasingly exposed to trauma, which can negatively affect their readiness to learn. If trauma disrupts children's ability to learn, then educators need to create classroom environments that can help children heal. Classroom culture—as adults are aware of children's emotions and respond compassionately to their dysregulation, fears, and isolation—becomes a mechanism to improve learning (Yu & Cantor, 2014). A classroom culture organized around consciousness, compassion, and community provides a buffer and a pathway to strengthen students' brain structures and behavior, enhancing the foundation that supports students' learning (Mason et al., 2018; in press).

Research has found that a highly effective method for alleviating anxiety is by engaging the heart's intelligence to increase *heart coherence*, establishing a smooth and balanced heart-rhythm pattern (Bradley et al., 2007). One way of incorporating all of these solutions is via yoga and meditation, which have been shown to help individuals become more aware of stressors and thus alter affective or physiological reactions (Kinser, Goehler, & Taylor, 2012). Yoga, mindfulness, and social emotional learning also increase compassion, which helps us cope with difficulties by understanding and "training" our emotions and reactions to others (Kirby & Gilbert, 2017).

By creating heart centered learners who support each other's academic and social emotional learning, schools will be shaping the whole child rather than just focusing on facts and knowledge. As Brené Brown (2015) said in her best-selling book *Daring*

Greatly: How the Courage to Be Vulnerable Transforms the Way We Live, Love, Parent, and Lead, "What we know matters, but who we are matters more."

CEI is implementing Heart Centered Learning (HCL) as part of a project with Yale University to help students who are at risk of developing mental illness. The project, the Childhood-Trauma Learning Collaborative (a component of the New England Mental Health Technology Transfer Center), involves use of HCL with its S-CCATE instrument in six New England states. As Larry Davidson, director of Yale's Program for Recovery and Community Health and director of the New England project indicates, "We envision a world in which no person will face discrimination and all persons be welcomed and valued for their strengths and the valuable contributions they make to the lives of their communities" (L. Davidson, personal communication, May 2019).

Dr. Susie Da Silva an assistant superintendent of education in Darien, Connecticut, and a member of the Childhood-Trauma Learning Collaborative, which is part of the New England Mental Health Technology Transfer Center, explains the vision of HCL and compassionate schools:

> *Tragedies across our nation's schools have empowered communities to rise and rally around the issue of mental health and how best to support students in the school setting. While school personnel are becoming smarter and studying deeper on topics related to social and emotional health, a vision for the future must include a wider net of professionals that can offer a comprehensive approach and understanding in and out of the school community. Mental health has been a topic that was ignored until recent year. Schools of now and schools of the future need to embrace and welcome supports into all of our schools, not just a select a few. Schools that are proactive and responsive, schools that begin and end with compassion. A place where adults care so deeply and are so transparent about mental health, that every member believes and feels that tending to their mental well-being is at minimum as important as every other academic area taught. Schools where adults teach through a heart centered approach, across every content area, across every component of the school day, this approach is without lesson plans or scripts, and is the*

> *"fabric" of each classroom. This isn't a lofty dream; it is within our reach. Together, we can break down the stereotypes, the misconceptions, and begin, where everything in life begins, with our hearts.*
>
> (S. Da Silva, personal communication, May 2019)

Recognizing the need for a tool to help teachers vision, plan, and monitor implementation of compassionate practices, CEI developed the S-CCATE, a validated forty-item tool to aggregate teachers' reports on perceptions of classroom and school culture (see Iterative Visioning in Chapter 4 of this book). With S-CCATE, teams of teachers use aggregated S-CCATE results to identify indicators for interventions and organize plans to improve conscious awareness and compassionate responses to students. As teachers focus on what they want to create in their schools, CEI's approach ensures that change is achievable and sustainable. We guide teachers to remove barriers to creating major change and sustainability in their classrooms as students' executive functioning improves. Unlike other social emotional learning or mindfulness initiatives, HCL relies on an iterative visioning and planning approach to stimulate systems thinking, shared vision, and creative tension.

With HCL, teachers (1) imagine the classrooms they want to create as they simultaneously increase their understanding (through our mindfulness practices) of the present reality of their classrooms and (2) envision improvements in consciousness, compassion, and community. Within a short space of time, this leads to creative tension, which teachers resolve by a guided iterative visioning process. Beginning with professional development and these visioning practices with teachers, CEI faculty guide learning teams of teachers and staff as they establish their own mindfulness practices and incorporate them in the classroom. Mason et al. (2018, in press) suggest that the following may be a path for implementation of HCL:

Implementing Heart Centered Learning

Phase 1—Planning

Meetings with parents, educators, and students to better understand needs. The meeting members will serve as a Core Learning Team.

The team will review the curriculum and provide guidance for the alignment of the SEL/HCL components with the existing curriculum.

Phase 2—Begin Implementation

Provide professional development and coaching. Begin with baseline assessments, including initial administration of S-CCATE. The project is also introduced to parents, who are invited to a series of informational meetings in conjunction with school activities to further their understanding of trauma, neuroscience, and HCL.

- Regular mindfulness practices, including deep breathing, rhythmic movement, yoga, focused attention, and body scans are used to integrate a child's mind and sensations in her or his body. Teachers will also learn to be more sympathetic and understanding in response to children's circumstances. As the classroom practices evolve, children become more calm and ready to focus and learn, leading to academic improvements.

- Teachers and students develop a shared vision of the classroom cultures they wish to create, share the collaborative plan, and engage students in two or three targeted goals to improve: (1) conscious awareness of self, including emotions and the impact of one's actions and attitudes on others; (2) compassionate thoughts and actions; (3) the EF involved in academic learning; and (4) building a nurturing, compassionate classroom culture supportive of students' readiness to learn. When teachers and students achieve significant success with one or two goals, they repeat the analysis of the classroom culture to identify new goals, reconsider their vision for the school, and repeat the cycle.

Phase 3—Infusing HCL With Academics

Following our curriculum, teachers will have guidance and opportunities to integrate HCL in ways that strengthen student compassion, confidence, and resiliency and also build a compassionate school culture.

The Importance of Visioning in Schools to Implement Heart Centered Learning

Dr. Michele Rivers Murphy, a coauthor with Dr. Mason, explains the importance of visioning this way:

My work facilitating the use of our envisioning tool, S-CCATE, paved the path for core learning teams to think beyond their own students' needs and classroom walls, with a wide-eyed lens of possibility and opportunity, extending to the greater good of the school community or whole. Systematic, transformational school change is a daunting proposition in parts. However, through the foundational practice of mindfulness combined with heart centeredness, something amazing unfolds. Visionary school leaders dare to exercise the courage to freely dream what if, while they simultaneously seek to support and develop others to do the same, realize their potential, maximize their contributions, and make an impactful difference on the overall common and collective good of the school community and beyond.

Visioning is a unique opportunity to cultivate, grow, and foster learning and whole school community environments that are compassionate, heart centered, and anchored by goodness. When the importance of interconnectedness is recognized, promoted, celebrated, and heartened, there becomes a mutual desire and willingness among the core learning team to encourage and empower one another with a sense of confidence that illuminates one's own abilities and potential, creating a real sense of purpose and school community of compassion. It is also this conscious, intentional and collective effort that organically drives their common and shared desire to make a profound and sustaining difference in the lives of their students through buffering the hurt, helping heal the wounds, and strengthening hearts so that hope and futures are realized.

(M. Rivers Murphy, personal communication, May 2019)

International Concerns and Children's Well-Being

Dr. Sharon Lynn Kagan, a pioneer in the world of early childhood policy; professor of early childhood policy at Teachers College, Columbia University, and Yale University; and co-director of the National Center for Children and Families is currently working with UNICEF to establish early learning standards in ten countries. Dr. Kagan has a unique voice in early childhood policy because she has worn many hats in the world of education. She began her career as a Head Start teacher, became a Head Start director, and then a superintendent for curriculum before entering in the public policy space. In her international research about high-performing early childhood systems, she describes the interface among cultural values, laws, regulations, policies, funding, and social change (Kagan, 2019).

Visioning and Educational Systems

Dr. Sharon Kagan
Co-Director, National Center for Children and Families
Teachers College, Columbia University & Yale University

Dr. Kagan's vision for early childhood education in America is "a system for young children that provides quality services for every single child, that distributes the resources equitably, and that is sustainable with services that are financially efficient."

When designing or redesigning an educational system, Sharon Kagan urges leaders to look not just at the programs their schools or district are implementing but also the infrastructure: "Think about regarding the entire district as one integrated system with many pieces. Identifying what the elements of the system are. There are different functions and you must understand each of them."

Dr. Kagan reminds us that systems work is difficult to accomplish unless the work being done in different, yet interlocking, areas of the system is happening simultaneously. First, break apart the system that exists to see how each element applies to the system as a whole. To effectively vision for change in your district, consider the following in conjunction:

- Standards and results

- Governance

- Financing

- Workforce

- Quality assurance

- Transitions

- Families and communities

When considering these elements, she advises that leaders keep in mind that the board of education is the governing body and often makes the final decisions, so it would be to a leader's advantage to help them understand the importance and benefits of systems building.

(D. Asby & S. Kagan, personal communication, May 2019)

An Entrepreneurial Vision for Education on a Global Scale

Kevin Simpson, founder of KDSL Global, an international organization providing professional development and technical assistance support in four different countries, describes how he worked with the Gulf Cooperation Council (GCC) to implement KDSL Global's vision for education:

> One thing we have learned is the need to have a personalized approach when working with a variety of countries and being flexible when change is needed. So over time we have embraced technology from using a blended approach, collaborated with the GCC ASCD, established a fellowship for educators, and shifted to working with startups and more education entrepreneurs.

> (K. Simpson, personal communication, May 2019)

Productive International Visioning

Kevin Simpson (2018) believes that an integral aspect of productive visioning is being present throughout the process. He provides some advice that may be useful as we consider educational trends:

> Wherever I'm at, I'm "on" for that time. When I was in Kuwait for just a week, I was really just "on" for Kuwait, even though there were so many other parts of the business clamoring for attention. I would push those things aside. This way of operating has roots in mindfulness and wellness. There are only so many things you can juggle at once.

When deciding which aspects of a school or district to change, he urges leaders to do a risk assessment. Ask yourself:

- Is it going to be worth it?
- Is it the right time?
- Are those taking the lead the right leaders?
- When your vision comes to fruition, what impact will it have on everything else?

(Continued)

(Continued)

Simpson advises leaders to read about their subject as much as possible:

> Don't just read about what is going on right now, but read about what could be. Hunt out any tips on what will come. I like reading about trends and patterns in education, and I always try to figure out what the article is not saying, too. What are they being silent on? What gaps exist?
>
> (Simpson, 2018)

Practical Points to Ponder

- What do you see on the horizon about trends that will support and/or possibly disrupt the vision you have for your school or district?

- How well resourced is your school or district for providing students access to and experiences with up-to-date technologies?

- Which of your programs are built on an understanding of neuroplasticity and students' brain development?

- How are changing demographics affecting your school or district? What action steps have you taken in response?

- Consider your electronic gadgets—perhaps the joy of instant communication, the reassurance that comes in the form of a text, the ability to record your life and set a digital display to music, all via a handheld device. How do these trends affect student skill sets and needs?

- How does your vision incorporate features that signal your school's or district's understanding both of the value and also the problems posed by technology?

- What can you do to strengthen the resources available to those in your school or district to ensure your students are prepared for the immediate and more distant future?

Ideas for Leading and Learning

- Nimbleness enhances our ability to adapt to change. Any organization will have those who are eager to be early adopters and others who are resistant to change—including being resistant to forces that are driving economies, setting the stage for the future, and sometimes even forcing us to spend hours ruminating over how to handle challenges that arise during the course of any month, season, or year. Who are your early adopters? How can you work with these individuals to help bring others along?

- However, moving forward needs to be balanced by a sense of purposefulness and some caution. Sometimes when we rush headlong into the future, we ignore warning signs that there will be more bumps in the road ahead. How do you set about balancing the desire to change and the lure of exciting possibilities with the need to be centered and focused?

- In this chapter we presented trends identified by *Forecast 5.0* as well as our own predictions for the future. Of all the trends discussed in this chapter, which do you believe will most affect your immediate future? How will you address these trends?

Resources to Explore

Scan the QR Code or visit https://resources.corwin.com/visioningonward to access live links to the online resources referenced in this chapter.

 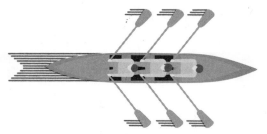

Chapter 9

CONCLUSION

> Problems cannot be solved by thinking within the framework in which the problems were created.
>
> —*Albert Einstein*

Dr. David Hornak, superintendent of Holt Schools in Lansing, Michigan, describes the importance of imagining a new future for education:

> Educators by nature are driven to serve others and solve problems. With that, we can no longer do school the way we have in the past. As a result, we need to imagine the possibility of serving our learning communities within a *new* framework. To that end, educators are desperately seeking to create a more flexible system where we innovate, educate, and inspire our learning communities to greatness on a daily basis. A system with more flexibility will produce critical problem solvers. We need to remove the barriers and get out of the way.
>
> (D. Hornak, personal communication, May 2019)

In *Visioning Onward*, we have attempted to provide an inspirational and pragmatic foundation for educational leaders to build upon as they drive innovation and readiness for the future with their local school communities. Knowing that each school has its own history and will want to chart its own course, we have strived to provide an array of examples from education, history, and business. In so doing, we have attempted to provide a compelling narrative for what we believe to be critical action that is urgently needed to lead schools into the future. We encourage you to work with teams to create, review, reflect, and strengthen your plans for your future. Figure 9.1 (first seen as Figure 0.2) depicts the steps we believe are critical prior to implementing your vision.

We have laid out the foundation for visioning and its steps in Chapters 1–6. In Chapter 7, we provided strategies for sustainability, including how to remove barriers and lay the groundwork for visions to last beyond the leadership that helped bring a particular vision to the forefront for a particular school or district. Visioning does not end with Step 8—after that step comes the need for developing a mission statement, goals, and an action plan.

To guide your work, we suggest that you highlight strategies from this text that you plan to use. In so doing, the content in Chapter 8 may

Figure 9.1   Implementing Your Vision: 8 Critical Steps

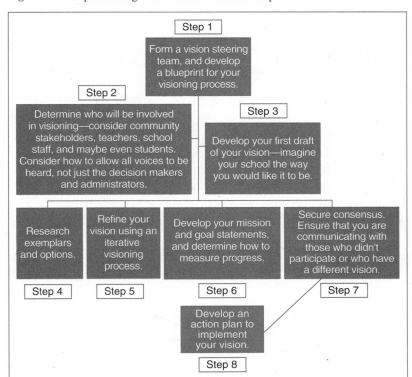

be useful in helping you consider trends in education and in the larger global community. As John Hattie says in *Visible Learning*:

> Transformational leadership refers to those principals who engage with their teaching staff in ways that inspire them to new levels of energy, commitment, and moral purpose such that they work collaboratively to overcome challenges and reach ambitious goals. . . . It is school leaders who promote challenging goals, and then establish safe environments for teachers to critique, question, and support other teachers to reach these goals that have the most effect on student outcomes.

(2009, p. 83)

Practical Points to Ponder

- Review the suggested eight steps to visioning. Where are you in the process?

- Where can you make headway most readily?

- If you could do one thing to strengthen your platform for progress, what would it be?

Leadership for Tomorrow

Although we are concerned about student outcomes, a recent post on a mindfulness LISTSERV by Ivan Sellers, an activist in mindfulness and heart centered learning and president of the Calm Mind Association in Portugal, helped frame our concerns. Ivan reminds us of the greater societal needs and the opportunities educators have to be part of an international solution.

Ideas for Leading and Learning

Life Tools

Ivan Sellers (personal communication, March 2019) explains one possible vision for the future of education:

Here in Portugal, over the last six months we have being using the social labs experiment of Otto Scharmer and the Presencing Institute of MIT to sense the educational system in Portugal. We have done this mainly through interviews. Our overriding conclusion is one of suffering. The educational system in Portugal, and I would venture that every educational system in the world, is full of suffering: students stressed, demotivated, resisting, and frustrated—teachers the same, schools directors the same, and parents with little time to intervene or follow but frustrated to see their kids struggling and/or in other cases adding to the pain. There are also small spots of light and well-being in the system.

Mindfulness is supposed to help teachers and students (and parents and everyone in the system who practices it regularly). But one thing is clear to most people who begin to practice mindfulness regularly is that it does not eliminate the need to also work on the pain one has inside, the trauma, and the triggers we all carry. For this, self-compassion is needed, therapy is needed, and nonviolent communication and emotional intelligence are needed. In this world-mindfulness becomes one of several instruments that all contribute to a healthier eco-system.

When we go out and teach *mindfulness*, we are teaching something that can obviously have an impact on one person's life, but in education it is the whole system that is begging for help. In our social lab, we are slowly coming to the conclusion that where mindfulness has a role is not through a mindfulness course per se but in bringing mindfulness silently into work that allows people in the system to listen to each other (active listening) and to talk to each other (generative dialogue). In these circumstances, mindfulness is not so much about a course as it is an instrument that need not even be named, that can be integrated in the process of listening and dialogue, and that will allow the educational system to begin to feel and be aware of its pain and start to address it and the system within which it exists.

It might be time to think of mindfulness not only as a course to present to the school but as a tool that can be used without formal teaching in all aspects of the school day and life.

- Where might mindfulness fit into your vision?

Resources to Explore

Scan the QR Code or visit https://resources.corwin.com/visioningonward to access live links to the online resources referenced in this book.

References

Accenture. (2000). Arthur Consulting announces a new name—Accenture—effective 01.01.01. Retrieved from https://newsroom.accenture.com/subjects/accenture-corporate/andersen-consulting-announces-new-name-accenture-effective-010101.htm

Accenture. (2016). *Accenture technology vision 2016: People first, the primary of people in the technology age.* Retrieved from https://www.accenture.com/t20160314T114937__w__/us-en/_acnmedia/Accenture/Omobono/TechnologyVision/pdf/Technology-Trends-Technology-Vision-2016.PDF

Accenture. (2018). Our history of innovation. Retrieved from https://www.accenture.com/in-en/accenture-timeline

Accenture. (n.d.). About Accenture federal services. Responsive strategic sourcing for services (RS3). Retrieved from https://www.accenture.com/us-en/insights/public-service/responsive-strategic-sourcing-for-services

Airasian, P. W. (1989). Institutional barriers to school change. In *High-school biology today and tomorrow* (pp. 252–265). Retrieved from https://www.ncbi.nlm.nih.gov/books/NBK218798/

Allegany County Public Schools. (2019). *Frost Elementary vision statement.* Retrieved from https://www.acpsmd.org/Page/1520

Alsher, P. (2015). The top 6 barriers to change and what change agents can do about them. *Implementation Management Associates.* Retrieved from https://www.imaworldwide.com/blog/the-top-6-barriers-to-change-and-what-changeagents-can-do-about-them

Amazon. (2019). Amazon culture and benefits. Retrieved from https://www.amazon.jobs/en/working/working-amazon

Amazon Web Services. (2019). AWS IoT button: Cloud programmable dash button. Retrieved from https://aws.amazon.com/iotbutton/

Arens, A. K., & Morin, A. J. S. (2016). Relations between teachers' emotional exhaustion and students' educational outcomes. *Journal of Educational Psychology, 108*(6), 800–813. http://dx.doi.org/10.1037/edu0000105

Ashoka Foundation. (2016, April 16). *Changemakers: Educating with purpose: By educators for educators.* Createspace Independent Publishing Platform.

Ashoka Foundation. (2017). *Everyone a changemaker: Shifting the conversation about education.* Sao Paulo: Author.

Ashoka Foundation. (n.d.). *Our theory of change.* Start Empathy website. Retrieved from https://startempathy.org/about/

Axner, M. (2018). *Chapter 14: Section 2. Developing and communicating a vision.* Retrieved from https://ctb.ku.edu/en/table-of-contents/ leadership/leadership-functions/develop-and-communicate-vision/ main

Bain, B. (2015, November 13). Why big history? Why the big history project? Why now? *National Council for the Social Studies.* Retrieved from https://blogdotbighistoryprojectdotcom.files.wordpress.com/2015/12/ bob-bain-handout-ncss-2015.pdf

Bainbridge, S. (2007). *Creating a vision for your school: Moving from purpose to practice.* Thousand Oaks, CA: SAGE.

Bakosh, L. S., Snow, R. M., Tobias, J. M., Houlihan, J. L., & Barbosa-Leiker, C. (2016). Maximizing mindful learning: Mindful awareness intervention improves elementary school students' quarterly grades. *Mindfulness*, *7*(1), 59–67.

Barrows, M., & Mason, C. (2018, March 8). A teacher's appeal to the heart: Does spirituality have a place in schools? [Web log post: Center for Educational Improvement]. Retrieved from http://www.edimprovement .org/2018/03/teachers-appeal-heart-spirituality-place-schools/

Bates, S. (2016). *All the leader you can be.* Columbus, OH: McGraw Hill.

Battelle for Kids. (2016). 21st century learning exemplar program. Retrieved from http://www.battelleforkids.org/networks/p21/21st-century-learning-exemplar-program

Beecher, M., & Sweeny, S. M. (2008). Closing the achievement gap with curriculum enrichment and differentiation: One school's story. *Journal of Advanced Academics*, *19*(3), 502–530.

Berg, J., Osher, D., Same, M. R., Nolan, E., Benson, D., & Jacobs, N. (2017, December). *Identifying, defining, and measuring social and emotional competencies. Final Report.* Washington, DC: American Institutes for Research.

Big History Project. (n.d.). *Summary of Big History Project research 2017/2018 school year.* Retrieved from https://school.bighistoryproject .com/bhplive

Blair, C., Zelazo, P. D., & Greenberg, M. T. (2016). *Measurement of executive function in early childhood: A special issue of developmental neuropsychology.* New York, NY: Psychology Press.

Blair, N. (2012). Technology integration for the new 21st century learner. *Principal*, *91*(3), 8–13.

Bradley, R. T., McCraty, R., Atkinson, M., Arguelles, L., Rees, R. A., & Tomasino, D. (2007). *Reducing test anxiety and improving test performance in America's schools: Results from the TestEdge National Demonstration Study.* Boulder Creek, CA: Institute of HeartMath. doi:10.1037/e503102012–001

Brown, B. (2015). *Daring greatly: How the courage to be vulnerable transforms the way we live, love, parent, and lead.* New York, NY: Avery.

Bryant & Stratton College. (2016). Instructor blog: The importance of reflection. Retrieved from https://www.bryantstratton.edu/blog/2016/july/instructor-blog-the-importance-of-reflection

Bryk, A. S., Sebring, P. B., Allensworth, E., Easton, J. Q., & Luppescu, S. (2010). *Organizing schools for improvement: Lessons from Chicago.* University of Chicago Press.

Burgess, S., & Houf, B. (2017). *Lead like a pirate: Make school amazing for your students and staff.* Dave Burgess Consulting, Incorporated.

Burrus, D. (2017). *The anticipatory organization: Turn disruption and change into opportunity and advantage.* Austin, TX: Greenleaf Book Group.

Cajete, G. (1994). *Look to the mountain: An ecology of indigenous education* (1st ed.). Durango, CO: Kivakí Press.

Canfield, J., & Switzer, J. (2005). *The success principles: How to get from where you are to where you want to be.* New York, NY: Harper Resource Book.

Castaneda, C. (2016). *The teachings of Don Juan: A Yaqui way of knowledge.* Berkeley: University of California Press.

Centers for Disease Control and Prevention (CDC). (2019a). About the CDC-Kaiser ACE study. Retrieved from https://www.cdc.gov/violenceprevention/childabuseandneglect/acestudy/about.html

Centers for Disease Control and Prevention (CDC). (2019b). Leading causes of death reports, 1981–2017. WISQARS™ Retrieved from https://webappa.cdc.gov/sasweb/ncipc/leadcause.html

Chakraverty, J. (2018, March 18). Companies' vision and values: Do they still matter? *Forbes.* Retrieved from https://www.forbes.com/sites/voicesfromeurope/2018/03/28/company-vision-and-values-do-they-still-matter/#769fd71c217f

Chang, Y. K., Chu, C. H., Wang, C. C., Song, T. F., & Wei, G. X. (2015). Effect of acute exercise and cardiovascular fitness on cognitive function: An event-related cortical desynchronization study. *Psychophysiology, 52,* 342–351. Retrieved from https://www.ncbi.nlm.nih.gov/pubmed/25308605

ChangeFactory. (2014). The components of a good vision statement [Web log post]. Retrieved from https://www.changefactory.com.au/our-thinking/articles/the-components-of-a-good-vision-statement/

ChangeFactory. (n.d.). Retrieved from www.changefactory.com.au

Christensen, T. (2015). *The creativity challenge: Design, experiment, test, innovate, build, create, inspire, and unleash your genius.* Adams Media.

Citizens Research Council of Michigan. (2019). Michigan's leaky teacher pipeline: Examining trends in teacher demand and supply. Retrieved from https://crcmich.org/PUBLICAT/2010s/2019/rpt404-teacher_pipeline .pdf

Clark, C. A., Pritchard, V. E., & Woodward, L. J. (2010). Preschool executive functioning abilities predict early mathematics achievement. *Developmental Psychology, 46*(5), 1176–1191. http://dx.doi.org/ 10.1037/a0019672

Clifford, C. (2017). These 14 billionaires just promised to give away more than half their money like Bill Gates and Warren Buffet. *Make It.* Retrieved from https://www.cnbc.com/2017/05/31/14-billionaires-signed-bill-gates-and-warren-buffetts-giving-pledge.html

The Collaborative for Academic, Social, and Emotional Learning (CASEL). (2018). Key district findings. Retrieved from https://casel .org/key-findings/

College Board. (2011). *Mission statements, strategic planning, and the college-ready district: A case study highlighting four Excelerator™ districts.* Retrieved from https://secure-media.collegeboard.org/digital Services/pdf/planning/MissionCaseStudyandProfiles_WEB%20 FINAL_102511.pdf

Cook, T. (2009). Apple vision statement. Retrieved from http://panmore .com/apple-mission-statement-vision-statement

Couros, G. (2015). *The innovator's mindset: Empower learning, unleash talent, and lead a culture of creativity.* San Diego, CA: Dave Burgess Consulting.

Covey, S. (1989). *The seven habits of highly effective people.* New York, NY: Free Press.

Daugherty, P. (2019). The post digital era is coming, are you ready? *Accenture.* Retrieved from https://www.accenture.com/us-en/blogs/ blogs-paul-daugherty-digital-transformation

Deloitte. (2019). 2019 global human capital trends. *Leading the Social Enterprise.* Retrieved from https://www2.deloitte.com/us/en/insights/ focus/human-capital-trends.html

DePaoli, J. L., Atwell, M. N., & Bridgeland, J. (2017). Ready to lead: A national principal survey on how social and emotional learning can prepare children and transform schools. A Report for CASEL. *Civic Enterprises.* Retrieved from https://files.eric.ed.gov/fulltext/ED579088.pdf

Dewey, T. (1897, January). My pedagogic creed. *School Journal, 54,* 77–80. Retrieved from http://dewey.pragmatism.org/creed.htm

Dintersmith, T. (2018). *What school could be: Insights and inspiration from teachers across America*. Princeton, NJ: Princeton University Press.

Dintersmith, T., & Wagner, T. (2015) *Most likely to succeed: Preparing our kids for the innovation era*. New York, NY: Scribner.

Disney, R. (n.d.). Brainy quote. *Xplore*. Retrieved from http://www.brainy quote.com/quotes/quotes/r/royedisne183365.html

Dolegui, A. S. (2013). The impact of listening to music on cognitive performance. Retrieved from http://www.inquiriesjournal.com/articles/1657/the-impact-of-listening-to-music-on-cognitive-performance

Dombo, E. A., & Sabatino, C. A. (2019). *Creating trauma-informed schools: A guide for school social workers and educators*. Oxford, UK: Oxford University Press.

Domenech, D., Sherman, M., & Brown, J. L. (2016). *Personalizing 21st century education: A framework for student success*. New York, NY: John Wiley & Sons.

Donaldson, T., & Preston, L. (1995). The stakeholder theory of the modern corporation: Concepts, evidence and implications. *Academy of Management Review, 20*, 65–91.

Donohoo, J. (2016). *Collective efficacy: How educators' beliefs impact student learning*. Thousand Oaks, CA: Corwin.

Donohoo, J., & Katz, S. (2017). When teachers believe, students achieve. *The Learning Professional, 38*(6), 20–27.

DuFour, R., & Marzano, R. J. (2011). *Leaders of learning: How district, school, and classroom leaders improve student achievement*. Bloomington, IN: Solution Tree Press.

Durlak, J. A., Weissberg, R. P., Dymnicki, A. B., Taylor, R. B., & Schellinger, K. B. (2011). Impact of enhancing students' social and emotional learning: A meta-analysis of school-based universal interventions. *Child Development, 82*(1), 405–432.

Dusenbury, L., Weissberg, R. P., Goren, P., & Domitrovich, C. (2014). *State standards to advance social and emotional learning: Findings from CASEL's state scan of social and emotional learning standards, preschool through high school*. Collaborative for Academic, Social, and Emotional Learning.

El Paso Independent School District (EPISD). (n.d.). EPISD 202 strategic plan. Retrieved from https://www.episd.org/cms/lib/TX02201707/Centricity/domain/4996/sel%20files/EPISD%202020%20No48.pdf

Fake, C. (2019). *Should this exist? Halo: A headset that makes you think faster.* [Podcast interview with Daniel Chao, cofounder and CEO of Halo Neuroscience.] Retrieved from https://shouldthisexist.com/halo/

Falken, A. S. (2012). *2012 U.S. Department of Education green ribbon schools*. Retrieved from https://www2.ed.gov/programs/green-ribbon-schools/closing-remarks-2012.doc

Falken, A. S. (2018). *Snapshot of 2018 U.S. Department of Education green ribbon schools.* Retrieved from https://www2.ed.gov/programs/green-ribbon-schools/closing-remarks-2018.doc

Farfan, B. (2017). Starbucks mission statement. Small business. Retrieved from https://www.thebalancesmb.com/starbucks-mission-statement-2891826

Feher, C. (2019). 10 K12 education trends to look for this year. *eSchool News.* Retrieved from https://www.eschoolnews.com/2019/02/06/10-k12-education-trends-this-year/

Flook, L., Smalley, S. L., Kitil, M. J., Galla, B. M., Kaiser-Greenland, S., Locke, J., . . . & Kasari, C. (2010). Effects of mindful awareness practices on executive functions in elementary school children. *Journal of Applied School Psychology, 26*(1), 70–95. doi: 10.1080/15377900903379125

Ford, M. (2015). *Rise of the robots: Technology and the threat of a jobless future.* New York, NY: Basic Books.

Freeman, R. E. (1984.) *Strategic management: A stakeholder approach.* New York, NY: Basic Books.

Frey, C. B., & Osborne, M. A. (2013). The future of employment: How susceptible are jobs to computerisation? *Technological Forecasting and Social Change, 114*, 254–280. Retrieved from https://www.sciencedirect.com/science/article/pii/S0040162516302244

Frey, N., Fisher, D., & Hattie, J. (2018). Developing "assessment capable" learners. *Educational Leadership, 75*(5), 46–51.

Fullan, M. (2011). *Six secrets of change.* Hoboken, NJ: Jossey-Bass.

Fullan, M. (2012). *Stratosphere: Integrating technology, pedagogy, and change knowledge.* London, UK: Pearson.

Fullan, M., & Quinn, J. (2016). *Coherence: Putting the right drivers in action.* Thousand Oaks, CA: Corwin.

Fullan, M., Quinn, J., & McEachen, J. (2018). *Deep learning.* Thousand Oaks, CA: Corwin.

Gabriel, J. G., & Farmer, P. C. (2009). *How to help your school thrive without breaking the bank.* Alexandria, VA: ASCD.

Galbraith, M. (2018). Don't just tell employees organizational changes are coming—explain why. *Harvard Business Review.* Retrieved from https://hbr.org/2018/10/dont-just-tell-employees-organizational-changes-are-coming-explain-why

Garcia, E., & Weiss, E. (2019, May 9). Low relative pay and high incidence of moonlighting play a role in teacher shortage, particularly in high poverty schools. *Economic Policy Institute.* Retrieved from https://www.epi.org/publication/low-relative-pay-and-high-incidence-of-moonlighting-play-a-role-in-the-teacher-shortage-particularly-in-high-poverty-schools-the-third-report-in-the-perfect-storm-in-the-teacher-labor-marke/

Gerver, R. (2013). *Creating schools that prepare for the future.* Retrieved from http://www.debats.cat/en/debates/creating-schools-prepare-future

Gerver, R. (2015). *Creating tomorrow's schools today: Education—our children—their futures* (2nd ed.). London, UK: Bloomsbury Publishing.

Gladwell, M. (2000). *The tipping point: How little things can make a big difference.* New York, NY: Little Brown and Co.

Gleeson, B. (2018). The critical role of leadership development during organizational change. *Forbes.* Retrieved from https://www.forbes.com/sites/brentgleeson/2018/06/04/leadership-developments-role-in-successful-organizational-change/#3289cc97fdd6

Goldman, S., & Zielezinski, M. B. (2016). Teaching with design thinking: Developing new vision and approaches to twenty-first century learning. In L. A. Annetta, & J. Minogue (Series Eds.), *Contemporary trends and issues in science education: Vol 44. Connecting science and engineering education practices in meaningful ways* (pp. 237–262). Springer Cham. doi.org/10.1007/978–3–319–16399–4_10

Grange Primary School. (n.d.). Vision, values, and aims. Retrieved from https://www.grangeprimaryschool.org/vision-values-aims/

Green, E. (2018, June 26). "Brain performance" firm DeVos invested in is hit for misleading claims. *The New York Times.* Retrieved from https://www.nytimes.com/2018/06/26/us/politics/betsy-devos-neurocore-brain-performance-ads.html

Greenberg, M. T., Brown J. L., & Abenavoli, R. M. (2016). *Teacher stress and health: Effects on teachers, students, and schools.* State College, PA: Robert Wood Johnson Foundation.

Gurley, D. K., Peters, G. B., Collins, L., & Fifolt, M. (2015). Mission, vision, values, and goals: An exploration of key organizational statements and daily practice in schools. *Journal of Educational Change, 16*(2), 217–242.

Habegger, S. (2008). The principal's role in successful schools: Creating a positive school culture. *Principal,* September/October. Retrieved from https://www.naesp.org/sites/default/files/resources/1/Principal/2008/S-O_p42.pdf

Hallinger, P., & Heck, R. H. (2010). Leadership for learning: Does collaborative leadership make a difference in school improvement? *Educational Management Administration & Leadership, 38*(6), 654–678.

Hanover Research. (2014). Best practices for school improvement planning. Retrieved from https://www.hanoverresearch.com/media/Best-Practices-for-School-Improvement-Planning.pdf

Hart High School. (n.d.). Vision and mission. Retrieved from https://www.harthighschool.org/apps/pages/index.jsp?uREC_ID=319400&type=d&pREC_ID=727780

Hattie, J. (2009). *Visible learning: A synthesis of over 800 meta-analyses relating to achievement.* New York, NY: Routledge Press.

Hattie, J. (2016). Mindframes and maximizers [Program]. Third Visible Learning Annual Conference: Washington, DC, July 11.

Heifetz, R. A., & Linsky, M. (2002). *Leadership on the line: Staying alive through the dangers of leading.* Boston, MA: Harvard Business School Press.

Hölzel, B. K., Lazar, S. W., Gard, T., Schuman-Olivier, Z., Vago, D. R., & Ott, U. (2011). How does mindfulness meditation work? Proposing mechanisms of action from a conceptual and neural perspective. *Perspectives on Psychological Science, 6*(6), 537–559.

Huang, L., Deng, Y., Zheng, X., & Liu, Y. (2019). Transcranial direct current stimulation with Halo Sport enhances repeated sprint cycling and cognitive performance. *Frontiers in physiology, 10.* Retrieved from https://www.ncbi.nlm.nih.gov/pmc/articles/PMC6383107/

Hudgins, E. (2011). *Secular spirituality* [Commentary at the Atlas Society website]. Retrieved from https://atlassociety.org/commentary/commentary-blog/4585-secular-spirituality

Hultman, M., Yeboah-Banin, A. A., & Formaniuk, L. (2016). Demand-and supply-side perspectives of city branding: A qualitative investigation. *Journal of Business Research, 69*(11), 5153–5157.

Kagan, S. (Ed.). (2019). *The early advantage 2—building systems that work for young children: International insights from innovative early childhood systems* (vol. 2). New York, NY: Teachers College Press.

Kaplan, R. S., Norton, D. P., & Barrows, E. A. (2008). *Developing the strategy: Vision, value gaps, and analysis.* Balanced Scorecard Review. Harvard Business School Publishing.

Katherine R. Smith Elementary School. (n.d.). About Katherine Smith. Retrieved from https://ksmithschool.eesd.org/page.cfm?p=3724

Kee, J. E., & Newcomer, K. E. (2008). Why do change efforts fail? *Public Manager, 37*(3), 5.

Kiersz, A. (2019, May 4). A lot of Americans are moving South—and many are heading to Florida. *Business Insider.* Retrieved from https://www.businessinsider.com.au/where-are-americans-moving-to-2019-5

Kinser, P. A., Goehler, L. E., & Taylor, A. G. (2012). How might yoga help. *Explore: The Journal of Science and Healing, 8*(2), 118–126. doi:10.1016/j.explore.2011.12.005

Kirby, J. N., & Gilbert, P. (2017). The emergence of the compassion focused therapies. In P. Gilbert, *Compassion: Concepts, Research and Applications*, Abingdon, Oxon United Kingdom: Routledge-Taylor and Francis, 258–285. doi:10.4324/9781315564296–15

KnowledgeWorks. (2018). *Forecast 5.0—The future of learning: Navigating the future of learning*. Retrieved from https://knowledgeworks.org/resources/forecast-5/

Kotter, J. P. (1995, May). Leading change: Why transformation efforts fail. *Harvard Business Review*. Retrieved from https://hbr.org/1995/05/leading-change-why-transformation-efforts-fail-2

Kotter, J. (2011). How to create a powerful vision for change. *Forbes*. Retrieved from https://www.forbes.com/sites/johnkotter/2011/06/07/how-to-create-a-powerful-vision-for-change/#1e83482d51fc

Kouzes, J., & Posner, B. (2009, January). To lead, create a shared vision. *Harvard Business Review*. Retrieved from https://hbr.org/2009/01/to-lead-create-a-shared-vision

Kouzes, J. M., & Posner, B. Z. (2010). *The truth about leadership: The no-fads, heart-of-the-matter facts you need to know*. San Francisco, CA: Jossey-Bass.

Kurz, T. B., & Knight, S. L. (2004). An exploration of the relationship among teacher efficacy, collective teacher efficacy, and goal consensus. *Learning Environments Research*, *7*(2), 111–128.

Leefeldt, E. (2018, August 21). America's rich are moving to the coasts as the poor go inland. *CBS News*. Retrieved from https://www.cbsnews.com/news/american-migration-rich-move-to-coasts-poor-to-the-heartland/

Leithwood, K., Harris, A., & Hopkins, D. (2008). Seven strong claims about successful school leadership. *School leadership and management, 28*(1), 27–42.

Leithwood, K., Seashore, K., Anderson, S., & Wahlstrom, K. (2004). *Review of research: How leadership influences student learning*. Minneapolis: University of Minnesota, Center for Applied Research and Educational Improvement.

Lemov, D., Woolway, E., & Yezzi, K. (2012). *Practice perfect: 42 rules for getting better at getting better*. San Francisco, CA: Jossey-Bass.

Levy, F., & Murnane, R. J. (2005). *The new division of labor: How computers are creating the next job market*. Princeton, NJ: Princeton University Press.

Lewin, K. (1946). Force field analysis. In *The 1973 Annual Handbook for Group Facilitators* (pp. 111–113). San Diego, CA: University Associates. Retrieved from https://www.worldcat.org/title/1973-annual-handbook-for-group-facilitators/oclc/9160197

Martin, R. E., & Ochsner, K. N. (2016). The neuroscience of emotion regulation development: Implications for education. *Current Opinion in Behavioral Sciences*, *10*, 142–148.

Marzano, R. J., & Waters, T. (2009). *District leadership that works: Striking the right balance*. Bloomington: IN: Solution Tree Press.

Mason, C., Rivers Murphy, M., Bergey, M., Mullane, S., Sawilowsky, S., & Asby, D. (2018). *Validation of the school compassionate culture analytic tool for educators* (*S-CCATE*). Vienna, VA: Center for Educational Improvement.

Mason, C., Rivers Murphy, M., & Jackson, Y. (2018). *Mindfulness practices: Cultivating heart centered communities where students focus and flourish*. Bloomington, IN: Solution Tree.

Mason, C., Rivers Murphy, M., & Jackson, Y. (in press). *Mindful school communities: The five Cs of nurturing Heart Centered Learning*. Bloomington, IN: Solution Tree.

Maxwell, J. (1995). *Developing the leaders around you: How to help others reach their full potential*. Nashville, TN: Thomas Nelson Inc.

Maxwell, J. (1999). *The 21 indispensable qualities of a leader: Becoming the person others will want to follow*. Nashville, TN: Thomas Nelson Inc.

McChesney, C., Covey, S., & Huling, J. (2012). *The 4 disciplines of execution: Achieving your wildly important goals*. New York, NY: Free Press.

McFalone, D. (n.d.). Live Well Lead Strong [Website]. Retrieved from http://livewellleadstrong.com

McKown, C. (2015). Challenges and opportunities in the direct assessment of children's social and emotional comprehension. In J. Durlak, C. Domitrovich, R. Weissberg, & T. Gullotta, *Handbook of social and emotional learning: Research and practice* (pp. 320–335). New York, NY: Guilford Press.

Medina, J. M. (2008). *Brain Rules: 12 principles for surviving and thriving at work, home, and school*. Seattle, WA: Pear Press.

Menasce, J., & Graf, N. (2019, February). Most U.S. teens see anxiety and depression as a major problem among their peers. *Pew Research Center*. Retrieved from https://www.pewsocialtrends.org/wp-content/uploads/sites/3/2019/02/Pew-Research-Center_Teens-report_full.pdf

Microsoft. (n.d.). Microsoft vision statement. Retrieved from https://bill-gates-waldhauer.weebly.com/goals-and-objectives.html

Milne, A. J., & Earl, T. R. (2010). *The new commonwealth schools: Creating the right school for your family and community*. Blackfoot, ID: Leadership Education Mentoring Institute.

MindTools Content Team. (n.d.). Forming, storming, norming, and performing: Understanding the stages of team formation. Retrieved from https://www.mindtools.com/pages/article/newLDR_86.htm

Mlodinow, L. (2018). *Elastic: Unlocking your brain's ability to embrace change*. New York, NY: Penguin Random House, LLC.

Nagy, J., & Fawcett, S. B. (2018). Proclaiming your dream: Developing vision and mission statements. Retrieved from https://ctb.ku.edu/en/table-of-contents/structure/strategic-planning/vision-mission-statements/main

The National Commission on Excellence in Education. (1983). *A nation at risk: The imperative for educational reform*. (Report to the Nation and the Secretary of Education, United States Department of Education).

Nettles, S. M., & Herrington, C. (2007). Revisiting the importance of the direct effects of school leadership on student achievement: The implications for school improvement policy. *Peabody Journal of Education, 82*(4), 724–736.

New York City Department of Education. (n.d.) *A vision for school improvement: Applying the framework for great schools.* Retrieved from www .teachersquad.com/uploads/5/8/2/0/58209821/avisionforschoolimprovement_applyingtheframeworkforgreatschools.pdf

Noddings, N. (2015). Back to the whole. In M. Scherer (Ed.), *Keeping the whole child healthy and safe.* Alexandria, VA: ASCD.

Nussbaum-Beach, S. (2011). A futuristic vision for 21st century education. *ASCD Express, 6*(11), 2015. Retrieved from http://www.ascd.org/ascd-express/vol6/611-nussbaum-beach.aspx

Nutt, A. (2018). Why kids and teens face far more anxiety these days. *The Washington Post.* https://www.washingtonpost.com/news/to-your-health/wp/2018/05/10/why-kids-and-teens-may-face-far-more-anxiety-these-days/

O'Connor, A., Blewitt, C., Nolan, A., & Skouteris, H. (2018). Using Intervention Mapping for child development and wellbeing programs in early childhood education and care settings. *Evaluation and Program Planning, 68*, 57–63.

Ontario Ministry of Education. (2014). *How does learning happen.* Retrieved from http://www.edu.gov.on.ca/childcare/howlearninghappens.pdf

Overstreet, S., & Chafouleas, S. M. (2016). Trauma-informed schools: Introduction to this special issue. *School Mental Health 8,* 1, 1–6. Retrieved from https://doi.org/10.1007/s12310–016–9184–1

Park View Elementary. (n.d.). Mission, vision, goals. Retrieved from https://www.parkview.simivalleyusd.org/missionvisiongoals

Perry, B. D. (2001). The neurodevelopmental impact of violence in childhood. In *Textbook of child and adolescent forensic psychiatry* (pp. 221–238). Washington, DC: American Psychiatric Press, Inc.

Perry, B. D. (2009). Examining child maltreatment through a neurodevelopmental lens: Clinical applications of the neurosequential model of therapeutics. *Journal of Loss and Trauma, 14*(4), 240–255.

Pew Research Center. (2019, June 12). Social media fact sheet. Retrieved from https://www.pewinternet.org/fact-sheet/social-media/

The Pickett Institute. (2002). *The power of visioning in strategic planning.* Institute for Law and Justice. Retrieved from http://ilj.org/publications/docs/Power_of_Vision_in_Strategic_Planning.pdf

Piper, P. (2019, July 10). The giving pledge, the plan to change billionaire philanthropy, explained. *Vox.* Retrieved from https://www.vox.com/future-perfect/2019/7/10/18693578/gates-buffett-giving-pledge-billionaire-philanthropy

Pipkin, C. (2015, December 27). How to craft an effective school improvement plan. *EdSurge News.* Retrieved from https://www.edsurge.com/news/2015-09-09-how-to-craft-an-effective-school-improvement-plan

Pratap, A. (2019, February 13). *How have technological changes affected businesses around the globe?* [Web log post]. Retrieved from https://www.cheshnotes.com/business/

Prince, K. (2017). The future of learning: Redefining readiness from the inside out. *KnowledgeWorks.* Retrieved from https://knowledgeworks.org/resources/future-learning-redefining-readiness/

Rainbow Community School. (n.d.). Holistic education. Retrieved from http://rainbowcommunityschool.org/about/seven-domains-2/

Rigaud, K., Kanta, A., Sherbinin, A., Jones, B., Bergmann, J., Clement, V., Ober, K., . . . & Midgley, A. (2018). *Groundswell: Preparing for internal climate migration.* Washington, DC: The World Bank. Retrieved from http://documents.worldbank.org/curated/en/846391522306665751/pdf/124719-v2-PUB-PUBLIC-docdate-3–18–18WBG-Climate Change-Final.pdf

Robert F. Kennedy Children's Action Core. (n.d.). Don Watson Academy vision & mission. Retrieved from https://www.rfkchildren.org/don-watson-academy/vision-and-mission/

Robinson, V. M., Hohepa, M., & Lloyd, C. (2007). *School leadership and student outcomes: Identifying what works and why* (vol. 41). Winmalee: Australian Council for Educational Leaders.

Rogers, S. (2015). *Where learning happens.* Teacherrogers website. Retrieved from https://teacherrogers.wordpress.com/2015/09/07/where-learning-happens/

Romem, I. (2018, April 3). Characteristics of domestic cross-metropolitan migrants. *BuildZoom.* Retrieved from https://www.buildzoom.com/blog/characteristics-of-domestic-cross-metropolitan-migrants

Samit, J. (2015). *Disrupt you!* New York, NY: Flatiron Books.

Schore, A. N. (2001). The effects of early relational trauma on right brain development, affect regulation, and infant mental health. *Infant Mental Health Journal, 22*(1–2), 201–269.

Schwab, K. (2017). *The fourth industrial revolution.* New York, NY: Crown Business.

Schwartz, P. (1996). *The art of the long view: Planning for the future in an uncertain world.* New York, NY: Currency Doubleday.

Semple, K. (2019, April 13). Central American farmers head to the U.S., fleeing climate change. *The New York Times.* Retrieved from https://www.nytimes.com/2019/04/13/world/americas/coffee-climate-change-migration.html

Senge, P. (2006). *The fifth discipline: The art and practice of the learning organization* (rev. ed.). New York, NY: Doubleday.

Senge, P. M., Cambron-McCabe, N., Lucas, T., Smith, B., & Dutton, J. (2012). *Schools that learn: A fifth discipline fieldbook for educators, parents, and everyone who cares about education.* New York, NY: Crown Business.

Sheninger, E. C., & Murray, T. C. (2017). *Learning transformed: 8 keys to designing tomorrow's schools, today*. Alexandria, VA: ASCD.

Silverthorne, S. (2002). The secret of how Microsoft stays on top. *Harvard Business School*. Retrieved from https://hbswk.hbs.edu/item/the-secret-of-how-microsoft-stays-on-top

Simmons, H. (2015). *Reinventing Dell: The innovation imperative*. Canada: Murmurmous Publishing Co.

Simpson, K. (2018). The KDSL global story: 10 lessons from an educational entrepreneur. *KDSL Global*. Retrieved from https://kdslglobal.wordpress.com/2018/03/01/10-lessons-from-an-education-entrepreneur-ebook-released/

Sinek, S. (2011). *Start with why: How great leaders inspire everyone to take action*. New York, NY: Penguin Random House.

Smith, M. K. (2001). *Peter Senge and the learning organization*. Retrieved from http://infed.org/mobi/peter-senge-and-the-learning-organization/

Spencer, J., & Juliani, A. J. (2017). *Empower: What happens when students own their learning*. London, UK: IMPress.

Starbucks. (n.d.) Starbucks company profile. Starbucks website. Retrieved from https://www.starbucks.com/about-us/company-information/starbucks-company-profile

Stein, L. (2016). Schools need leaders—not managers: It's time for a paradigm shift. *Journal of Leadership Education, 15*(2). Retrieved from https://eric.ed.gov/?id=EJ1131961

Stollznow, K. (2011). Healing and harming sounds. *Skeptic Magazine*, 16(4) Retrieved from https://www.skeptic.com/eskeptic/11–12–07/#feature

Strategic Business Leader. (2008). *Developing a shared vision*. Retrieved from http://www.fasttrackplanning.com/developvision.html

Supovitz, J., Sirinides, P., & May, H. (2010). How principals and peers influence teaching and learning. *Educational Administration Quarterly, 46*(1), 31–56.

Swoveland, M. (2013, December 4). Where learning happens. *Teaching Tolerance*. Retrieved from https://www.tolerance.org/magazine/where-learning-happens.

Takayama, T. (2018). *3D printers: A buyer's guide* [Web log post]. Retrieved from https://www.iste.org/explore/Toolbox/3D-printers%3A-A-buyer

Tanner, C. (2015). *The creativity challenge: Design, experiment, test, innovate, build, create, inspire and unleash your genius*. Adams Media.

Team ISTE. (2015, April 17). *8 ways to establish shared vision* [Web log post]. Retrieved from https://www.iste.org/explore/Lead-the-way/8-ways-to-establish-shared-vision

Thoits, P. A. (2010). Stress and health: Major findings and policy implications. *Journal of Health and Social Behavior, 51*(S), 541–553. doi: 10.1177/0022146510383499

TopNonprofits. (2017). *30 example vision statements.* Retrieved from https://topnonprofits.com/examples/vision-statements/

Tuckman, B. W. (1965). Developmental sequence in small groups. *Psychological Bulletin, 63*(6), 384–399. Retrieved from http://dx.doi.org/10.1037/h0022100

University of Kansas Center for Community Health and Development. (n.d.). Community tool box. Retrieved from ps://ctb.ku.edu/en/table-of-contents/structure/strategic-planning/vision-mission-statements/main

U.S. Department of Education (DOE). (2017, January 19). Improving outcomes for all students: Strategies and considerations to increase student diversity. Retrieved from https://www2.ed.gov/documents/press-releases/improving-outcomes-diversity.pdf

U.S. Department of Health & Human Services, Administration for Children and Families, Administration on Children, Youth and Families, Children's Bureau. (2018). *Child maltreatment 2016.* Retrieved from https://www.acf.hhs.gov/sites/default/files/cb/cm2016.pdf

Walkley, M., & Cox, T. L. (2013). Building trauma-informed schools and communities. *Children & Schools, 35*(2), 123–126.

Washington County Public Schools. (n.d.). Our schools. Retrieved from http://wcpshr.com/our-schools

Webber, J. (2018, December 13). Honduran farmers flee effects of climate change. Financial Times. Retrieved from https://www.ft.com/content/adc270e2-fd72–11e8-aebf-99e208d3e521

Yu, E., & Cantor, P. (2014). Turnaround for children, poverty, stress, and schools: Implications for research, practice, and assessment. *Turnaround for Children.* Retrieved from http://www.turnaroundusa.org/wp-content/uploads/2016/05/Turnaround-for-Children-Poverty-Stress-Schools.pdf

Zelazo, P. D., Carlson, S. M., & Kesek, A. (2008). The development of executive function in childhood. In C. A. Nelson & M. Luciana (Eds.), *Developmental cognitive neuroscience. Handbook of developmental cognitive neuroscience* (pp. 553–574). Cambridge, MA: MIT Press.

Index

Leadership That Makes an Impact

LYN SHARRATT

Explore 14 essential parameters to guide system and school leaders toward building powerful collaborative learning cultures.

MICHAEL FULLAN

How do you break the cycle of surface-level change to tackle complex challenges? *Nuance* is the answer.

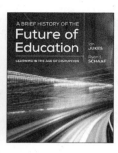

IAN JUKES & RYAN L. SCHAAF

The digital environment has radically changed how students need to learn. Get ready to be challenged to accommodate today's learners.

ERIC SHENINGER

Lead for efficacy in these disruptive times! Cultivating school culture focused on the achievement of students while anticipating change is imperative.

JOANNE MCEACHEN & MATTHEW KANE

Getting at the heart of what matters for students is key to deeper learning that connects with their lives.

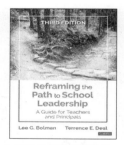

LEE G. BOLMAN & TERRENCE E. DEAL

Sometimes all it takes to solve a problem is to reframe it by listening to wise advice from a trusted mentor.

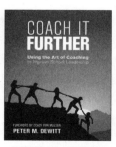

PETER M. DEWITT

This go-to guide is written for coaches, leaders looking to be coached, and leaders interested in coaching burgeoning leaders.

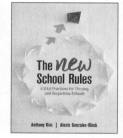

ANTHONY KIM & ALEXIS GONZALES-BLACK

Designed to foster flexibility and continuous innovation, this resource expands cutting-edge management and organizational techniques to empower schools with the agility and responsiveness vital to their new environment.

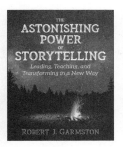

LDN191J1

A SAGE Publishing Company

CORWIN HAS ONE MISSION: to enhance education through intentional professional learning.

We build long-term relationships with our authors, educators, clients, and associations who partner with us to develop and continuously improve the best evidence-based practices that establish and support lifelong learning.